ADVANCE PRAISE FOR
REDEFINE YOUR SERVANT LEADERSHIP

"Jon Kidwell writes with authenticity and vulnerability, both hallmarks of servant leadership. Jon has written a recipe for creating servant leadership that is unique to you and the leadership role you inhabit."

— **Paul McEntire**, formerly COO, YMCA of the USA and CEO of the YMCAs in Houston and Jacksonville

"This book is magnetic and pulled me into it immediately. As leaders, we get caught up in certain beliefs about leadership — easy to do with the multitude of resources available on the subject. One thing became clear for me: we do not assess our own behaviors, thoughts and principles often enough to make sure we are being the servant leaders we want to be – with intention. This book makes you look deep into yourself and gives you the roadmap for validating where you are on that journey. Jon gives you the practical tools for doing so and the guidance to become a true servant leader. I was inspired by his willingness to share his personal story and journey so we could all learn from it."

— **Melinda 'Mel' Underhill**, Chief Volunteer and Human Resource Officer Houston Livestock Show and Rodeo

"This book is an 'amplification' of Jon's life! In *Redefine Your Servant Leadership* Jon provides insights on how each of us, guided by our values and faith, can discover our optimal balance of Character, Relationships and Skills that will let us humbly go 'all-in' as Servant Leaders of our families, communities and businesses."

— **Mark Houser**, former Energy Executive and Founder of Symphero Energy Solutions

Redefine
YOUR SERVANT LEADERSHIP

Amplify Your Integrity, Influence, and Impact

JON KIDWELL

LEAD*Well*

First Published in the United States in 2024 by Leadwell

Cover Design & Illustration: E.J. Schiro, Schiro Creative
Interior Layout: Carolyn Oakley, Luminous Moon Design + Press

For permission requests, please contact:
Leadwell, 11805 Chimney Rock Rd. #35874, Houston, TX 77035
hello@leadwell.com

Publisher's Cataloging-in-Publication
(Provided by Cassidy Cataloguing Services, Inc.).

Names: Kidwell, Jon, author.

Title: Redefine your servant leadership : amplify your integrity, influence, and impact / Jon Kidwell.

Description: Houston, TX : Leadwell, [2024] | Includes bibliographical references.

Identifiers: ISBN: 979-8-9896716-0-1 (paperback) | 979-8-9896716-1-8 (ebook)

Subjects: LCSH: Servant leadership. | Leadership--Religious aspects--Christianity. | Success in business. | Management--Religious aspects--Christianity. | Career development--Religious aspects--Christianity. | Self-actualization (Psychology)--Religious aspects--Christianity. | Motivation (Psychology) | BISAC: BUSINESS & ECONOMICS / Leadership. | BUSINESS & ECONOMICS / Personal Success. | RELIGION / Christian Living / Professional Growth. | RELIGION / Christian Living / Personal Growth.

Classification: LCC: HD57.7 .K54 2024 | DDC: 658.4092--dc23

To servant leaders everywhere who tirelessly work to help others.

CONTENTS

INTRODUCTION

You've likely heard about servant leadership. It may even be your answer to the common interview question, "Tell us about your leadership style." You have experienced the connection created by being a servant leader, felt the pressure of it, and reluctantly accepted or relentlessly pressed on, even when it pains you personally, because of your heart for people and devotion to the meaningful work you do.

I commend you. I am you. That is why I wrote this book.

I am Jon Kidwell, founder and leader of Leadwell, a leadership development company. Visit www.redefineyourservantleadership.com for a message from me. Plus you'll get access to digital resources to supplement this book.

I have always been fascinated by leadership, and this book is the result of my personal and professional journey as a leader, business owner, teacher, volunteer board member, husband, father, and leadership coach. It is a reflection of my successes and failures, my insights and discoveries, my sorrows and joys. It is also the combination of the principles and practices I learned along the way.

You see, there came a point where the way I led as a servant leader, and what I believed servant leadership to be, was no longer serving me, my team, or my organization. I was confused. Frustrated. Honestly, I was crushed. So much of what I prided myself on as a leader fell as quickly as a Jenga tower near a two-year-old.

In this book, we will look at how we define leadership, how it defines us, and how we need to redefine servant leadership to achieve even greater results and serve people at an even greater depth. We will realign ourselves around the three attributes servant leaders need, replace ten common myths and misconceptions about servant leadership, and walk you through simple steps to reinforce your leadership transformation. This process will give you the strong foundation you need to lead, the support to lead at your best, and the confidence and skills to deliver amazing results. You will have the tools and see the path to amplify your integrity, influence, and impact to make a tremendous difference in your work, in the world, and your life.

I hope this book will inspire you, inform you, and transform you. I invite you to join me on this journey and redefine your servant leadership. I challenge you to apply the principles and practices that you will learn in this book. I call on you to act as a leader. To serve first, to always serve, and to serve in all ways. I believe that this is the best way to lead, and the best way to live. I believe that this is the way to change the world, one leader at a time.

Are you ready?

Let's begin where it nearly ended for me...

DEFINED

A belief that your qualities are carved in stone leads to a host of thoughts and actions... a belief that your qualities can be cultivated leads to a host of different thoughts and actions, taking you down an entirely different road.

— *Mindset* by Carol Dweck[1]

DEFINING MOMENTS

"Jon, can I talk to you for a second?"

There are times this phrase is light and jovial. This wasn't one of those times. My boss at the time asked me this question following a semi-impromptu team meeting. Immediately, I could feel my body tensing up: the slow constriction of muscles, the increasing clammy-ness of my palms, and the slight shake in my hand. The right hand more than the left. We didn't even sit down. We made it inside the door, then he turned and looking down at me said,

"Jon, I know you are an honest person. But, your inability to engage in conflict and share what you're thinking in these meetings makes me, and others, question your integrity. You need to make a change and engage honestly with us or you won't be a part of this team."

I quietly coughed out, "Okay," before excusing myself to the painfully slow elevator ride before fumbling to get into my car and finally collapsing into my hands on the steering wheel. I was devastated. I worked so hard to get to this leadership position only to be told I was failing — and people thought I was dishonest at that. *How could this be? I am proud to be a person of integrity. I was nice to everyone. I helped out, stayed late, came in early. I was respectful and never talked back. I would bite my tongue. I didn't lie. I worked hard to fix problems. I was the first to take on new responsibilities, projects, and initiatives. I managed our finances and cut back if we needed to. I motivated people to do more and try harder. I was making a difference. I mean come on, considering some people's work, how they do it — and they're questioning me?! For goodness' sake, I am a servant leader. I am someone who serves and keeps the peace, and never argues. Can others say they do that?*

In one 12-second conversation my integrity, my influence with my boss and my peers, and my ability to continue to lead, to serve, to make an impact was on the line. Heck, my entire identity was challenged. No, it was threatened. As a servant leader, I prided myself on my integrity, on how I treat people, and on delivering impactful results. I kept thinking what am I going to do? Is he right?

LEADERSHIP DEFINED

The very first leadership conversation I remember having was with my dad. I was about twelve years old. We were driving home from one of my activities. I can't remember the activity, but the conversation stuck with me. I was asking my dad about one of the other dads who took up a lot of the air in the room. You might say he was loud, pushy even. My question wasn't as clear then as I write it here, but I asked him if that man was in charge. I'll never forget what my dad said: "You don't need to be the loudest one in the room to be the leader." "You don't have to be the loudest one in the room" made sense to me — even at twelve — that this guy's loud, pushy demeanor made people feel uncomfortable. My dad's wisdom combined with my intuition laid a foundation for leadership.

I discovered I had a knack for *leadership*. I had many opportunities to lead after that day, and would combine what my dad taught me with my own personality and what I was learning about leadership. I was involved in student government and the captain of sports teams. I was on the Youth Leadership Council for my church. I co-founded a club for my major in college. I gravitated toward situations where I could fill in the gap, do things others couldn't (or wouldn't) do, and lead by example. I was never the most popular, the best athlete, or the smartest. What I did was live out what I thought leadership was the best way I knew how: help people do things, serve them, and act like you are supposed to act, while leading by example. Especially since I wasn't going to be the loudest in the room, these two things, serving others and leading by example, came in handy. And they worked. I realized that this type of leadership will get good results and always bring you an abundance of opportunities to lead.

Do you ever get three hours into a project, putting together a child's toy, or setting up your electronics and think, "Gosh, I really need to read the instructions?" That's what happened to me as I continued to take on various leadership roles. I thought, "I don't actually know what I'm doing. How am I actually supposed to do this leadership thing?" So I did what any young research-averse individual does. I Googled it. Here's what I found as the most popular entries for leader and leadership:

> **Leader:** *the person who leads or commands a group, organization, or country* (Google.com)[2]
>
> **Leadership:** *the office or position of a leader* (Merriam-Webster)[3]

You don't need a title to lead. There is no secret handshake.

You begin to lead when you act.

You earn the opportunity to continue when you

act in a way that serves others.

The loud, pushy approach started to make sense. The idea behind the stereotypes and stories about bad bosses were making a lot more sense. I discovered we almost purely define how a leader acts and who they are by two of the things that bother us most about leaders — a commanding style and a focus on hierarchy. How can these foundational beliefs not in some way define, or at least influence, how we lead? I knew I didn't want to lead that way. I had enough bad bosses and good examples to know this wasn't going to be how I did it. I went with my instincts, and the good examples of others — I thought "I am sticking with serving people and leading by example."

Eventually, I realized there was a whole philosophy behind this type of leadership. It's called servant leadership. I began to round out what I thought it meant to be a servant leader through my experiences and my personality, by talking with others, from the others' comments on my leadership, and by reading books. This is what I came to understand about servant leadership. It is a leader who serves. They care about the people. Since they care, they are nice, pleasant, and in good spirits. They don't go around telling people what to do, they are the ones giving help, and showing the way. Focusing on keeping the peace and helping people. They work for the benefit of things greater than themselves — for community, for good causes, for the benefit of others. They may not be the best (probably aren't) but they will work harder, stay later, and be available to help whenever needed. It isn't about the money for them. They don't have to be the ones in charge and don't make themselves appear to be even when they are. Servant leaders are honest. They do good things, for good reasons.

Now, I wouldn't dare to say I nailed the definition of servant leadership, especially in my late teens and early twenties. I will say that I pretty much nailed my definition of servant leadership. The attitude, actions, and approach I thought were necessary to lead and to be a servant leader began to define how I led. And, my definition plus my ability to do that definition "perfectly" definitely defined how I judged myself as a leader. The more I aimed to live out my definition of servant leadership, the more I realized the challenges of doing so.

What if I'm not nice?
Or in good spirits?
What if I need help?
We need money to run our organization, so why do I feel so bad focusing on it?

I wasn't ready to give up on what I thought it meant to be a servant leader. I didn't want to be a boss. You know a loud, commanding, position and power-driven person where it is all about them. Plus, I was finding success with my approach. I have too much evidence from my success and the people in my life reinforcing my beliefs of how a servant leader should act to want to make a change.

REINFORCED BY SUCCESS

When something works, we often do it again. Heck, we even try to reinforce and amplify that success by taking it one step further or teaching someone else to do it like we do it. We tend to look for information to support our point of view, even when there may be evidence that contradicts it. That was exactly what happened to me — just on steroids. In ten years, I went from teaching elementary school physical education to being a vice president in a $100+ million organization — leading thousands of people and serving hundreds of thousands of people. Leading as a servant worked. Leading by example, saying yes where others wouldn't, caring deeply, working really hard, and helping people was the key. My success was the evidence I needed that my approach worked. And, I had plenty of instances (and opinions) that reinforced it.

"The most important thing in leadership is integrity," said my principal at the school where I first taught. Honesty was critical for her. This was fuel for my fire. It confirmed that living up to the perfect ideal was important. It reinforced my high moral and ethical standards. It cemented the belief that honesty and trust are key virtues for us as humans, but especially for leaders. And, I felt it was easy enough to deliver on — I always felt like I was operating honestly and with integrity. *Don't we all?* The more honest I was, the more trust I earned, and the more opportunities I was offered.

There's this movie, *Yes Man,* where Carl, played by Jim Carrey must say "yes" as a part of a covenant with the universe because if he says no it will go poorly.[4] This was my understanding of what it meant to serve and to lead — you say "yes." And by golly, it worked. Saying yes led to opportunities, even in the first year of my career, to develop a district-wide curriculum, join task forces, and train tenured teachers. After teaching, and working for the YMCA, it led to leading projects, joining committees with senior leaders, promotions that bypassed tenured team members, and to taking on leadership roles in parts of the entire organization — not just one location. I saw that saying yes, and always being available, was a great way to serve and gain opportunities to lead. It makes sense, right? It isn't very nice to say no, and servant leaders are nice people, *right?*

"Oh, Jon. Yeah, he's such a nice guy!" Hey, you attract more flies with honey than vinegar. Am I right? Saying "yes" helped reinforce that nice guy persona, too. Being seen doing things like picking up trash, holding doors, parking far away, and being the first to respond to emails does too. But, few things bring success and reinforce you're a nice person like solving other people's problems. Treating people well and solving large, complex financial and people problems is what I tell people earned me seven promotions in six years. Going wherever and picking up jobs no one really wanted, implementing technological solutions that save people time and the organization millions, turning around business units financially and culturally, and consistently outperforming budgeted goals reinforced my style and amplified my success.

The trouble was, I didn't feel successful.

I was helping the organization do better financially. I made more money than I thought I would in my early 30s as a result. I had the title and was considered a "rising star." While I looked very successful professionally, personally, I felt like a fraud. I was being honest — but not completely.

I would stop when it got to the part you didn't want to hear and I didn't have the courage to say. My words and actions said it was all about the people, while my decisions were aimed at primarily the business's financial interests. I was saying "yes," even if I thought saying "no" was the right call. Then I'd rationalize scenarios and decisions in my mind saying "it's not that bad" or "they don't care as long as they get the result they want."

I took on those jobs and solved those problems but created other problems for myself and others. I broke commitments to my family. Bit off more than I could chew. Confused team members we fired because instead of being clear about expectations I wanted them to be happy and like me. I realized I was a really good do-er, but maybe not the leader I thought I was. Even with all the people I led, I was solving the problems. I was taking on and taking over problems my team brought to me. Simply because I liked helping, wasn't patient enough, and struggled to hold them accountable. I had a problem. I had gone full servant — subservient even — but I was not leading for fear of being a boss, and it was crushing me.

My boss was right. My skewed view of servant leadership and personal limitations were destroying my integrity, dismantling my influence, and diminishing my impact. How did it come to this? And how did I end up so far from where I was trying to go?

AMPLIFIED BY CULTURE

Have you ever been told something so many times you start to believe it? Even if it goes against what makes sense in your heart and mind? Once you state, "I am a servant leader," there are interpretations, perceptions, and expectations that come with that. Expectations that you have a big heart, are humble, helpful, and care about people. Those are good and right. There are other, false, narratives about who and how a servant leader must be that confuse, limit, and burn people out. These false narratives about servant leadership turn them off to the entire idea of servant leadership because of the cognitive dissonance created by impossible standards, contradictory messages, and practices that do not serve or produce the results they, and others, need to succeed.

This is how I felt: guilty for missing the mark, compelled to please people, and overwhelmed by my desire to help... everyone... and "look good" doing it was keeping me from actually doing it. Sure, there were instances of leading in the tension of what the business needs and treating people well, engaging in conflict, and holding others to expectations. None of us are ever completely one way or another. None of us are completely People-Pleasers or completely Self-Serving — it is a spectrum.

But, on the whole, I had released the tension and fell to one side because of what I believed about servant leadership. I found these narratives came from two places. The media and the people closest to me. One shaped my perception, the other my practices. Let's start with the ones that hit closest to home. And that is what people, especially people close to you, say to you about servant leadership.

I live in Texas. We say "bless your heart." There are two types of "bless your heart." The kind that conveys you care. And the kind that conveys "Oh, you sweet little thing. You have no idea how this actually works." The latter is the kind I received a lot, especially from supposedly "successful" people and business leaders. The proverbial pat on the head indicating, "That's nice that you care, work hard, and do meaningful work — but that's not how it works in *real* business or life. A business is about profit. If you *really* want to

The *shoulds* are heavy for servant leaders.

Should-ing reinforces perfectionism,

ratchets up the fear of negative responses,

and piles on the social pressure.

succeed, to lead, you need to… (insert any statement that indicates treating people unfairly is okay because It's Just Business and we all get it)."

I can't speak for others, but I have interviewed and coached enough to know this isn't just a me thing. The looking down on individuals and industries — education, nonprofits, ministries, female-owned businesses to name a few — belittles the people and the good work they do. They feel boxed in, like they must choose. People or profit. Service or success. This is crippling the impact and effectiveness of the serving professions.

What other words, phrases, or expectations do the people say that amplify the disconnect between what servant leadership is and what we make it out to be? Phrases like (each of these were said to me or shared with me):

→ That wasn't very nice. I thought servant leaders were supposed to be nice.

→ If you really cared you'd stay late.

→ I thought we were a family. Families wouldn't fire someone.

→ Oh, I see. You talk the talk, but when it really comes down to it you're just like everyone else. (Firing someone for repeatedly underperforming)

→ I can't believe you told me this wasn't good enough. That wasn't very nice. (For turning in a project late)

→ When did you start thinking you were better than anybody else? (For not attending a function)

The *shoulds* are heavy for servant leaders. A very effective method to get what you want short-term is *should-ing*. Telling people what they should do guilts them into submission. *Should-ing* reinforces perfectionism, ratchets up the fear of negative responses, and piles on the social pressure.

In spite of the challenges servant leaders face from people closest to them, the philosophy of servant leadership has gained popularity again in recent years. Its resurgence is tied to the rise of self-directed teams, extremely agile organizations where a project manager may lead without authority, and non-hierarchical or flat organizations. With that has come interpretations and guidance from leadership and business people, and media outlets. This second influence, media, impacted my perception of servant leadership.

The problem is, when the message is incomplete or inaccurate the megaphone of a media outlet not only reinforces what is not true, it embeds that ideal in the culture and lexicon of the people trying to achieve it. Two examples that sum up how this became evident to me in recent years were in Forbes and Society for Human Resources Management (SHRM) articles. Let's dive into each to see how the incorrect or incomplete narrative hurts servant leadership and the leaders who aspire to lead this way.

First, the Forbes article titled, *Traditional Leadership vs. Servant Leadership.*[5] While the article doesn't clearly indicate a winner between the two, it is clear that if you want to succeed in business as we know it — enter servant leadership at your own risk.

In the article it states in, *"a traditional leadership approach, the leader encourages people to do their jobs by providing them with guidance, direction and motivation. The main focus of a traditional leader is to improve the business position of the company or the organization in the market."*[5] Okay. I can see that. And, at the same time, I am not quite sure how that might differ from servant leadership.

The article goes on to say the following about servant leadership, *"Servant leadership occurs when the leader's main goal and responsibility is to provide service to their people."*[5] And this is where limiting belief and either-or narrative is driven home. This article, and others like it, reinforce that serving is the goal, not the natural approach in service of the goal.

However, it is the next sentence that really closes the door on servant leadership being a path to leading at the highest level and serving both people and performance. *"A servant leader focuses on the people that are directly below them, rather than the company as a whole."*[5] The message, intended or not, is that as a servant leader you cannot do both — service and strategy. People and performance. You cannot lead at the highest level because then you need different goals and have different concerns. This further separates the servant from the leader in the mind of the leader.

To further drive home the point that if you want to succeed as a leader in the business world, it likely can't be as a servant leader, because, as the article goes on to say, performing servant leadership perfectly is the only option:

"Ethics have become an important concern in the business environment. Various research is being done on servant leadership, and the leaders who implement this style of leadership should make sure it is done honestly and ethically. A wide range of different scales have been created to measure the magnitude of servant leadership and ethics in various organizations. These scales were created because although servant leadership may have numerous positive aspects, its downside is that if the leader does not behave ethically, then practicing servant leadership for the benefit of the organization is pointless and a far-fetched idea." [5]

Does this mean we expect traditional leaders to behave unethically? I should hope not. Yes, of course, behaving unethically is terrible and harms people and organizations. But it is potentially just as harmful to turn people off from trying to integrate a service-oriented approach to doing good meaningful work in a way that produces results, including profits, for the people and the place.

Second, an article published on SHRM titled, *What is Servant Leadership: A Philosophy for People-First Leadership* is a good article.[6] The only thing wrong with this article is a *one-degree off* concept that leads to a world of difference. The article's title states it. *"A philosophy for people-first leadership."* What is wrong with that you may ask? First, if I remember right, I think *The Servant as Leader* by Robert K. Greenleaf was about a servant-first philosophy, not people-first philosophy, so we'll get to more on that shortly.[7] Second, and it is so slight it could be missed, if you put people first, the whole thing falls apart. This is what I mean by a *one-degree off* idea. It starts off as a small problem in definition or understanding but if you follow it to the end — you find you arc way off target, and way off your path.

The small but enormous difference is that servant leadership has to be in service of something greater than any one person — it must start with a mission. A mission is more permanent. A mission can withstand scrutiny. And a mission is compelling to everyone involved. If people are first, we focus too much on the short-term wants, desires, and requests of people, not the highest priority needs of all people involved and the work we do together. Servant leadership must start with a mission. A mission-first approach, especially one that is ultimately aimed at helping people, creates the environment where we can humble ourselves in service to said mission, and strive to serve people always, not just first.

You know the final, and maybe most perilous thing that amplifies all the myths about servant leadership? Me. You. What we tell ourselves without even uttering a word. The soundtracks that loop in our head over and over again. Those stories we tell ourselves of how it has to be and if you are really like this then you will only do that. The promises we make with ourselves. The "I will nevers" of our mind. The efforts to release the tension of the hard work it is to lead and to serve and keep ourselves from ever, even accidentally, falling over the cliff of being bossy, just about business, or only in it for the money.

I got to the point where I was sick of having my leadership defined by others. I was tired of allowing myself to be defined by others. I was exhausted trying to please everyone, and feeling like I was pleasing no one. I was done beating myself up for feeling guilty every time I made a good, even right decision, because it might not be the one others want. I saw other leaders, successful leaders, servant leaders even, and there was something positively different about them. They were humble, successful, respected, strategic, and service-oriented. I wanted to know what they knew. I was ready to redefine myself as a leader. **Are you?**

REDEFINED

Part of the problem is that serve and lead are overused words with negative connotations. But they are also good words and I can find no others that carry as well the meaning I would like to convey. Not everything that is old and worn, or even corrupt, can be thrown away. Some of it has to be rebuilt and used again. So it is, it seems to me, with the words serve and lead.

— The Servant as Leader by Robert K. Greenleaf[7]

WHAT IS SERVANT LEADERSHIP?

I knew there was a better way. A way to be a great leader who cares, who is devoted to a mission *and* grows a successful business, who grows people, and a vibrant community dedicated to the mission. Leaders who dare to speak the hard truth. Leaders who rigorously built and empowered teams while also making seamlessly impossible decisions, even firing people, still approached the work with humility, love, compassion, strategy, boldness, and service. Leaders like this also say, "I am a servant leader."

How in the world do they stand so strong in the tension of what seems so contradictory? Things like people and performance. Authority and compassion. High standards and an unmatched level of humanity. How in the world do they lead *AND* serve? What do they know that I don't? And what is servant leadership, really?

I went back to Merriam-Webster. I didn't like what I found before. Maybe defining "servant leadership" will be better. Nope! Not even an entry in the dictionary. While you can find suggestions for what you might have meant — serpent eagle, rain leader, and squad leader — there is nothing for servant leadership. I had to dig deeper and really do my research. Now, even though I present it here quickly, this was a journey of discovery, application, and growth over several years.

I began where the modern philosophy of servant leadership began, with *The Servant as Leader* by Robert K. Greenleaf. Greenleaf asks if servant and leader can be fused into one person and calling. He examines a man named Leo from Herman Hesse's *Journey to the East* who is seen first as a servant, but discovered later as a noble leader. Greenleaf shares the servant-leader who is servant-first begins with the natural feeling that one wants to serve *first*. Then that awareness brings one to aspire to lead. This combination leads to making sure people's highest priority needs are being served. Ultimately sharing power, putting the needs of others first, and helping them develop and perform as highly as possible.[7]

You likely know, as I did, many of the characteristics of servant leaders Greenleaf outlined. Attributes like listening, understanding, healing, and empathy. Traits like foresight, awareness, and acceptance. Plus, a focus on community. These are well-known, put-on posters, and plastered on social media. It is easy to see how pulling these out might influence leaders like you and me to approach servant leadership like I did. What I discovered rereading *The Servant as Leader* blew me away.[7]

Perhaps like me, you didn't know, or remember, that Greenleaf also talks about performance, persuasion, withdrawal, power, and authority. He outlines that servant leaders always accept the person, but sometimes refuse to accept effort or performance as good enough. He is clear that a servant leader is decisive and directs the way we must go to achieve the goal. That this leader is confident, even more than their followers. That even as a servant they must withdraw to serve one's self to be of service to others. Greenleaf shares that servant leaders don't avoid power and yet do not use coercion. Rather, they use power to create opportunities and greater autonomy for the people they serve. These discoveries completely dismantled my one-sided view of servant leadership as subservient and are in direct opposition to the cultural narrative of just being nice. Greenleaf's actual work goes against the idea you solely focus on the care of your team and that you can't tell people no.[7]

These discoveries, and my natural inclination for all things *leadership,* led me further into what servant leadership is. In quick fashion, here are many of the snippets I found that led me to see not only servant leadership, but all leadership, as I do.

In *The 21 Irrefutable Laws of Leadership,* John Maxwell states that leadership is influence. Nothing more, nothing less. He doesn't say influence is merely getting people to like you, from your charisma, or based on a position but that influence is earned from a combination of character, relationship, knowledge, intuition, experience, success, and ability.[8]

In response to the fear of self-centered leadership becoming the norm Patrick Lencioni wrote *The Motive* where he outlines reward-centered and responsibility-centered leadership approaches. He argues for the responsibility-centered approach and says that this responsibility brings one to develop people, align their actions, behaviors, and attitudes, have difficult conversations, run great meetings, and communicate constantly. He also states that leadership is an action, not a position. That all leadership is in fact, servant leadership.[9]

Among countless other books, I turned to a place I often turned to for wisdom, the Bible. I saw things each of us may already know. Ideals like, "[...] *those who are last will be first, and those who are first will be last."* (Matthew 20:16) *"Do for others what you want them to do for you."* (Matthew 7:12) I began to see and appreciate concepts differently than before. Things like, *"Love must be completely sincere. Hate what is evil, hold on to what is good."* (Romans 12:9) One leader I learned more about was a Jewish King named David.[10]

King David relentlessly sought to stay on mission. He saw his God-given purpose as serving and honoring God by leading Israel. Above all else, he strived to do just that. He references that mission often. When he would go into battle — it was to serve and honor God by leading Israel. When he avoided battle — it was to serve and honor God. His mission-first approach led to the reunification of the two Jewish kingdoms, Israel and Judah. The land and wealth of Israel grew exponentially during David's reign, so much so that his son, Solomon, who would have been trained by and inherited everything from David, is often referred to as the wealthiest and wisest man ever. I found a verse (Psalms 78:72) that references how David led Israel.

Where true service exists, there will be love.

Where true love exists, there must be service.

It says, *"[He] took care of them with <u>unselfish devotion</u> and led them with <u>skill</u>."* Once again, I was pointed back to serve and to lead, together, as the path. To embrace the tension that it is — to be able to lead well.[10]

I needed a new definition, not one focused on position, power, or control. Not a circular narrative that a servant leader serves. I needed something that could help me, and others, aspire to more as leaders. A definition that helps us achieve service to that highest priority need.

A NEW DEFINITION

Trying to fit new attitudes, thoughts, and behaviors into the old system of leadership (command, position, title) required a new definition. I needed to avoid the overused and unclear words like "serve," but it needed to draw one to that ideal. It needed to include purpose, people, and performance as these are core of all leadership. I tested and scrapped variations for years. At a point of frustration, thinking I may never land on something that might work, I chose to do what is often best when stuck. Act.

I humbly submit this new definition of servant leadership to you:

Servant leadership is the act of influencing the attitudes, thoughts, and behaviors of others toward a shared purpose.

You don't need a title to lead. You don't need status. It's not something you're born into. And there is no secret handshake or special position that makes you a leader. You have the opportunity to lead. Where you are. With the people around you. To do great things. For great causes. Today. You begin to lead when you act. You earn the opportunity to continue leading when you act in a way that serves others.

You earn even more opportunities and influence as others see and experience your character, relationship, knowledge, intuition, experience, success, and ability related to the work you do. Influence gives you the ability to impact the lives of others, to impact their attitude, to shape how they think, and to direct their actions toward a shared purpose. But, beyond who and how you are, above everything else actually, the one thing that builds influence most is love. Love is the greatest level of service one can offer another. Love, as I define it for our discussion here, is *the very act of the will for the benefit of another.*

This love shows up as love for the people and the mission. It amplifies a leader's influence. It enables us to lead people and not to force, demand, or coerce. It invites others to follow, to join in a shared purpose where their skills and talents are in the service of something greater than each of you, or any of us. The purpose, the very reason you lead, serve, and work tirelessly is what unites, inspires, and compels each of us to place this mission first. To love people. To *always serve, and serve all ways.*

IMPACTFUL RESULTS

I know what you're thinking, "Trust but verify." Even though I am starting to buy what you're selling, even though I'm frustrated, stretched thin, tired of feeling guilty, and just want to lead like I believe is needed and know I can… I need some proof that this challenge, this leaning into the tension of being a humble servant and strong leader won't backfire, that this new approach to servant leadership will really grow my team, my organization, and me.

Earlier, I shared about my seven promotions in six years. I shared with you this feedback from my boss. *"Jon, I know you are an honest person. But, your inability to engage in conflict and share what you're thinking in these meetings makes me and others question your integrity. You need to make a change and engage with us or you won't be a part of this team."*

Now, I look back on this moment that cracked my perfectionism and my sense of myself as a successful leader, and I am deeply grateful. I am grateful to a leader who had the courage to put our purpose ahead of my momentary happiness and to tell the truth and help me grow.

Redefining my servant leadership sped up my growth and produced even better results for me and for the organization. The department turnarounds and consistently outperforming multi-million-dollar annual budgets came after I redefined my servant leadership. My first promotion took two years. The next six happened in four years, all while leaning into and leading in the tension of serving and leading in a *mission first, people always* approach.

Where you might expect employee engagement and retention to drop, the opposite happened. My team stayed longer and performed better. The best part, better than any tangible results. I was free. Free to speak the truth, kindly. Free to say "yes." To say "no." I freed myself to communicate expectations and hold people to what they agreed to because it was good for the business *and* their growth. I was free to delegate, to decide, to use my talents, and to invite others to contribute theirs. I was free to lead. To serve. To be me.

It isn't just me. Leaders who redefine servant leadership and live it produce results. They build $600+ million-dollar organizations benefiting their community, their teams, and good causes all around the world. They change the culture of entire nations for the better. They lead well — integrating purpose, people, and performance for truly impactful and lasting results.

This is what we help our clients do at Leadwell. Through coaching and training we help leaders grow themselves, align their teams, develop leaders, and build winning cultures. We coach leaders, and teams of leaders, through the process outlined in the rest of this book to grow their impact. In training, we give teams and organizations the skills and practices needed to deliver impactful results. In their organizations they increase employee engagement and retention, they create more aligned and mission-driven teams, and increased financial performance. Results like a YMCA that grew top-line revenue *over* 25% (millions of dollars) in 2 years. And as a result could increase wages, expand and improve existing services, and ultimately serve more people.

In fact, we have countless examples where embracing the tension of serving *and* leading grows the organization's bottom line and the well-being of the people. Like when a CEO saved the organization from a hostile takeover because she embraced reality and asserted the need to the board. Or, when a new CEO wanted to change the culture from working all hours, lots of late nights and weekend texts, and pestering, aggressive tirades if something went wrong to a culture of performance, collaboration, with a better work-life balance. We have had the privilege to see how each leader (and organization) has grown, changed, and created a different future for themselves, their teams, and the world.

It's time for you to redefine your servant leadership. To realign on what's needed and replace the myths that do not serve. So you can amplify your integrity, influence, and impact. To produce the impactful results that serve your organization, your team, and you.

REDEFINE YOUR SERVANT LEADERSHIP

As Greenleaf said, the servant as leader takes care to make sure the highest priority needs are being served. The highest priority for us right now, the biggest need, is to develop ourselves into servant leaders with the Character, Relationships, and Skills to create the outcomes and changes we want in our work and our lives. Why? Because your impact grows when you do. Your integrity grows when you have the ability to lead in and through real and challenging circumstances. Your impact grows when your needs are met and you extend your focus to the mission, serving people, and looking for ways to make an even greater difference through your life and work.

Now that we've redefined servant leadership in a principled, practical, and productive way, we are going to move on to the how. This book will take you through the *how* of growing ourselves to live and lead as servant leaders. We will first look at, and realign on, the three aspects of servant leadership: Character, Relationship, and Skills — but not as individual areas of growth. We see these as the three interrelated areas where we can integrate and lead well.

Then, we will work together to replace the myths that exist about servant leadership and servant leaders so they no longer limit our attitude and approach to acting in ways that truly serve and grow the people and places we lead.

Those will be the tasks of the next few sections of the book. Once we have laid the foundation, we'll move on to how to reinforce this growth and change for lasting results in ourselves and in others. And, finally, we'll focus on how to amplify your servant leadership and what to do to truly create exponential impact where you lead, as well as around the world, to develop stronger, service-oriented leaders, and create healthy, thriving organizations, communities, and movements that have the possibility of truly changing the world.

REALIGN

Do not be conformed to this world, but be transformed by the renewing of your mind.

— Paul of Tarsus[11]

THREE KEY ATTRIBUTES FOR SERVANT LEADERS

We just redefined servant leadership as the act of influencing the attitudes, thoughts, and behaviors of others toward a shared purpose. While this book focuses primarily on "professional" leadership, leading a business, organization, or team. The principles apply to all aspects of life. To your marriage, as a parent, in your neighborhood, where you volunteer… anywhere. Not only do they apply, they enhance, refine, and mutually support each other. To be one way at work and a completely different way at home or as a community leader leaves you conflicted and everyone else confused.

I discovered the same for the attributes people would ascribe to servant leaders. What would you say is the most important attribute of a servant leader? Most often I hear, "It's their character." Others say, "No, it really is about how they treat people. It's about relationships." And still, others would say, "They need the skills to get the job done. Servant leaders serve — they do. They have to be able to get it done." Let me tell you, it isn't one or the other. It is the integration of the three — Character, Relationships, and Skills — that servant leaders need.

Compartmentalizing is not living wholly. If you're not living wholly you can never hope to be living holy. (I couldn't help myself — it's quite punny.) But it's also true. Showing up holy and wholly are the same. As I engaged with life, and team members, I continuously found a deficit in Character, Relationships, or Skills led to a disingenuous exchange or the inability to do what my team or the business needed done. If leaders don't continuously integrate and grow in all three areas, they end up with a Dr. Jekyll and Mr. Hyde approach where they act very differently at different times. Leaders need to be who they are at work, at home, or with their neighbors, or at the grocery store. They also benefit, and the team benefits when they are consistent in their approach across circumstances. If we try to compartmentalize, eventually, the armor becomes too heavy or it cracks. That's when it all falls apart because being a different person in different places is not a productive way to hold tension or be human.

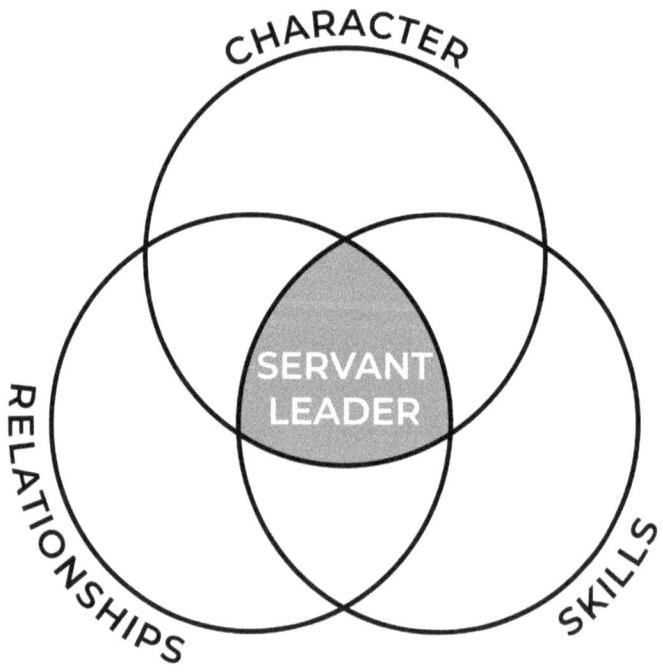

One might consider the main focus of the leadership coaching business would be about work. While that may be, life does not cleanly separate itself. Just as *serve* and *lead* may seem like an oxymoron, really there is an overlap and even an integration of the two. Same goes for work-life and life-life. The more integrity you develop to walk with through life, the more influence you gain in the people and the places that you find yourself. You have Skills, and the more you are able to see them as applicable in all facets of your life, the more useful you are to others. Servant leadership just works everywhere.

BUILD A STRONG, INTEGRATED FOUNDATION

Servant leaders need to develop three attributes to lead with integrity, grow their influence, and increase their impact: Character, Relationships, and Skills. All three are essential to being an effective and impactful leader. Character calls us up. Relationships keep us from falling. Skills drive impactful results. If we don't have all three, we end up not just hindering our influence, our integrity, and our impact, we actually work against it.

If we are extremely strong in Character, but we have meager Relationships, and poor Skills? Well, all of a sudden, we become extremely self-righteous, because we have extremely high standards, very good principles and morals, but we fail to show up and do what we say. We rationalize, intellectualize, or we don't have the Skills to put things into action. We become great morally idealistic theorists, and this creates distance between us and other people. We are hypocritical or we become delusional and in either case, our Character stands in our way.

If we are very good at Relationships, but don't have good Character or Skills, we are great with people. But, without the moral and ethical compass, we run the risk of being a manipulator. And without the Skills, we are not consistent in our delivery. Navigating relationships can become highly political, because our internal compass of right and wrong, of what's needed in this situation is ticking all over the place, dependent on what's in it for me and not the purpose I am seeking to advance. Relationships alone can put us in a place where we become highly manipulative, because we can move so well through being able to be there for people that we call them to act and do things that might be best for us and not best for them.

Skills alone with no Character and low Relationships lead us to driving really fast and hurting people or leaving people behind, including ourselves. If I have the Skills to deliver and I have the drive, but have not stopped to question whether we should do this or that, it can end up taking people and organizations in the wrong direction. The lack of relationship and bond with the people we work with and for leads to a diminished care and compassion. These folks most often show up as distant executives who are highly Skilled, highly trained, very driven, good hearted, and yet disconnected from reality — and become misdirected as a result.

To download the Character, Relationships, Skills diagram, visit www.redefineyourservantleadership.com.

Right now, grab a piece of paper. Draw the three circles diagram. Label it. If you don't have any paper, then write on the three circles diagram in this book. Think about which attribute is your strongest attribute today. Maybe even the one you over-index on. Put a star by it. How about the one that needs the most growth and attention right now? Put a triangle, a delta sign, by that one. Think about these as you read through this section and begin your growth journey as a servant leader.

The key to redefining servant leadership comes down to growing these three attributes: Character Relationships, and Skills — together. Like the tension of serving and leading, the tension of growing and leading through your Character, Relationships, and Skills brings the balance needed to lead well. Plus, it's good to have your eggs in more than one basket. A cord of three strands is not easily broken. You become more resilient and versatile as a leader when all three areas get some attention. When you have Character, Relationships, and Skills, you can apply these together differently in different situations because you want to stack them. However, when we talk about developing the three attributes, we do need to talk about them one at a time or we will get overloaded. So, hold the tension of them being inseparable as we separate them to make sense of them.

I have three kiddos and we play Jenga a lot. Jenga is so cool (and frustrating) because like life and leadership, you spend way more time building the Jenga tower than it takes to knock it down, especially with children. Usually with kids, it's two moves in and the game is over. Then we take the time to re-stack it all together again. The other thing about when you're stacking a Jenga tower is that you can't just put three on three on three on three on three, all in the same pattern. Right? If they are all parallel, as soon as you take one out, the game's over. However, if you put the pieces in a cross stitch or a perpendicular pattern, three left, three right, three straight, all of a sudden the tower is stronger. Character, Relationships, and Skills are a Jenga game. If we cross hatch them in a pattern, we get the support we need to keep the game going. When we have all three attributes going strong, it can give us some grace when we, or other people, mess up. We can withstand a few knocks and get things back in balance. Unlike Jenga, in the game of servant leadership, we can put blocks back in and others can fill the gaps with their blocks too.

Let's build these foundational blocks for you to redefine your servant leadership. In this chapter we are going to dig in and focus on building Character, Relationships, and Skills as servant leaders.

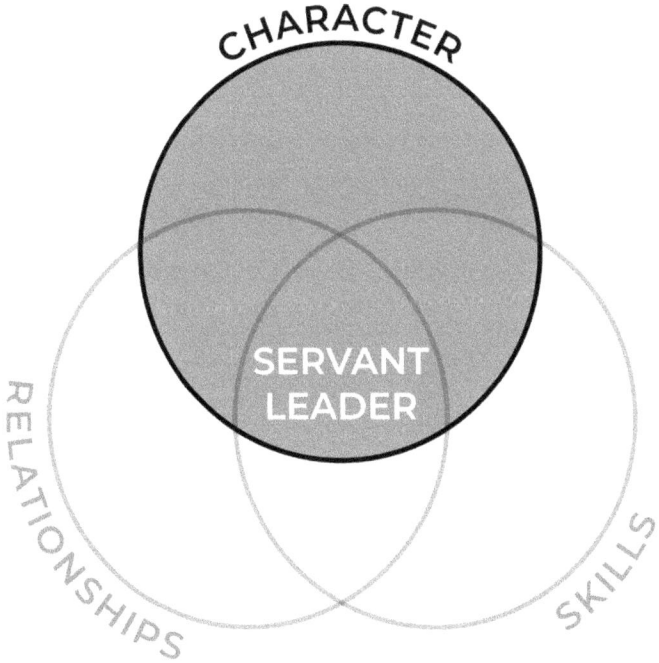

CHARACTER

When we think of Character, we often think of someone with high moral and ethical standards, someone who has guiding principles, someone who is a good human. Through Dr. Henry Cloud's book *Integrity,* Dr. John Townsend's Institute at Concordia University Irvine, and their joint project, *Ultimate Leadership,* I was introduced to the idea that *Character is the ability to meet the demands of reality.*[12] It isn't just my moral code, Character is who I am and how I am — especially when the demands are high. As a leader, you know the demands are often high.

In our diagram on the previous page, Character is on top. Our Character pulls or calls us up, and is our ability to rise to the occasion. Before diving into the aspects of building a strong Character I learned through Dr. Cloud and Dr. Townsend, let's start with the first part of Character, the part we all assume makes or breaks our Character — that is our morals, ethics, and values. For all of us, but especially as leaders, it is important for us to be clear on these because they will influence our actions and drive decisions we make, and decisions and actions of the people we lead. Use these questions to help yourself identify your core morals, ethics, and values.

→ What code or compass guides my view of right and wrong?

→ Where do I get those values and beliefs?

→ What am I willing to defend and "lose the battle" over but won't give up my belief?

→ What ideas and values anchor me in hard times?

→ What ideas and values influence my decisions and actions greatly?

→ What are some non-negotiable behaviors or beliefs I live by?

→ What values or guiding principles do you follow to live in personal integrity?

→ In what situations do I find myself living outside of my desired values or norms?

→ How do these get lived out in my life and leadership?

When we work with leaders, we guide them through these questions to help them identify personal or organizational values. Then, we begin to weave bigger themes and patterns together and simplify to a small number of values or guiding principles. Once you identify what is of utmost importance to you, whether you go to personal experience, the Bible, psychology, another religious book, or other teachings, then you can begin to live by those principles. We all need something greater than ourselves by which we navigate life and work. We can rise above what's best for me and begin to act on what is best in general. That's when we can begin to ask how to live by those principles, over time, consistently.

How do we show up and embody Character consistently? These values and guiding principles are only as good as the degree to which they influence our actions. Left on a sheet of paper, or merely adhered to when convenient (or worse in one's own mind), will not produce the type of Character we need to succeed in leadership. Through Cloud and Townsend's *Ultimate Leadership* program, Cloud's book *Integrity,* and my time teaching at the Townsend Institute at Concordia University, I learned essentials for building strong Character. They outline them, for counseling programs, and for leaders, as attachment, separation, integration, and adulthood. (For further study, check out Dr. Cloud's book *Integrity* and/or Dr. Cloud's and Dr. Townsend's book *Boundaries.*) Here is how I practically summarize them: a) make and maintain healthy relationships, b) set boundaries, c) accept the good and embrace the bad, and d) emotional and positional maturity. Let's explore each of them.[11]

MAKE AND MAINTAIN HEALTHY RELATIONSHIPS.

"No, I've got this. I can do it by myself." "I am the one who does the helping. Not the other way around." "Oh no, I don't want to burden you with what I'm going through." Each of these statements have been uttered by me. Maybe you too. Each statement is also an indicator for a Character shortfall because of a lack of healthy relationships. We will dive more into Relationships next. For now and for our Character development let's focus on our need to make and maintain healthy relationships where we can share needs, feelings, and commit to and rely on others. When we rely on others to help meet needs, know and honor our feelings, and when we can commit to do the same for others we gain the freedom to be honest with people, the support to deliver on life's challenges, and the perspective as a leader that we need be able to truly commit to what is best for the mission and the people we lead.

I get it. There is a stereotype that leaders have to have it altogether. Have all the answers. That if you accept help you are selfish. That if you, especially you as a leader make a mistake, it will discredit all you've done. The idea that if you share how you really feel you will be judged. Or, that you don't get to show emotion because people need to know you're confident. The pervasive thought that the natural distance and separation of having leadership responsibilities means I don't get "my peeps." And that that is good because then I can make the decisions I need to make because I am a bit detached. I get each of the thoughts and rationales. I also get that each of these stereotypes of strong Character are in fact the obstacle to having legitimately strong Character as a leader.

It was August 2017. Hurricane Harvey was devastating Houston. I was standing in 6 inches of water. In my house. I was grateful my wife, Meghan, and 4-month-old daughter, Anna, were not in Houston. Between activating a bunch of staff and volunteers for the YMCA's response, moving anything still dry to the next second floor, and checking in on neighbors I was exhausted. I vividly remember sitting on the roof of the condo watching a woman be airlifted out of her home by a Coast Guard helicopter and sleeping upstairs with 8 inches of water in the house and all the noises that came with plugged up plumbing.

So, there I was standing in the condo and my now-mentor, Preston, called me. "How you doing, Jon?" He already knew. Shortly after the pleasantries he shared that his wife Susan and he had space to welcome two families into their home. He offered Meghan, Anna, and me the opportunity to stay with them while we figured out what to do and repair our home. How generous! My response, while standing in water up to my ankles, was "Thanks. I think we're okay, if something comes up, I'll call you." How stupid of me. It was a painful, eye-opening experience that exposed my inability to make and maintain healthy relationships grounded in giving *AND* receiving, sharing feelings, and to commit to and rely on others. I was quietly isolating myself and trying to do too much by myself at home, in life, and definitely as a leader at work.

It took me a couple of days, but I called him back, broken down and crying, and asked if the offer was still there. He said, "Yeah." And I said, "Okay, I'll see you tomorrow." The next four months living in one house with three families (six adults, three kids, and two dogs) taught me the value (and absolute necessity) of healthy relationships. These Relationships produce even stronger Character not through perfection, but through the growth and joy that comes when you experience mutual giving and receiving, people who understand and honor your feelings, and where people can commit to honestly act for the benefit of each other. This love, yes love, reduced stress, built an awareness and increased compassion for others who face challenges. Through love, I learned receiving is good and can actually be a way to serve others by allowing them to serve you. It is this love that gave me the support I needed to be able to lead and serve my family, the families I lived with, and my work through that challenging time.

I don't recommend flooding your house, but nothing exposes character like a crisis. Look for areas you are reluctant to receive help, share what's really going on, and connect with people in an honest and heartfelt way. I understand that you can't and won't do this with everyone, but find some and begin to ask for help, share your struggles or challenges, and stay connected with a person or group of people through thick and thin — when you do it will produce a better understanding of how to then provide that for others, build it into the culture where you lead, and operate with greater integrity because you do not need to shoulder it all alone.

SET BOUNDARIES

"Okay, I'll leave in 10 minutes" inevitably leads to helping 10 more people and getting home an hour after you said you would. This might be a trivial example (until it happens every day for a year), but what about boundaries on who you are and who you're not. Have you ever found yourself being someone or doing something completely outside of your character to avoid making someone else angry or having to say no? The ability to meet the demands of reality, consistently over time, requires that you set and keep boundaries.

Boundaries give you the power to honor your commitments. To align with your values. To live and lead as who you are and how you desire to, especially when it is important that you do so. To operate with integrity as a person, and especially as a leader you have to be able to say "No," you have to be able to say "Yes," and you have to be able to say and value that "You are you and I am me." Being able to clarify: this is right, this is wrong, this is in, this is out is an act of setting and maintaining boundaries. Boundaries are like water when poured in

We must
learn to be independent

before others can depend on us,

and we can
depend on others.

a glass. Inside the glass the water is contained and can be easily drunk. Water poured on a table is a mess. If you don't have boundaries, there is no way to live out your values and principles because you are just weaving your way through the things that are most easy, most convenient, or most pressing at that moment. Without boundaries you lose the ability to be trusted, respected, and to deliver as expected, consistently over time.

Imagine you work in a nonprofit that responds to the needs of people in your community. The requests you receive for help have to do with meeting real needs of people and children. Needs like food, water, shelter, clothing, and care. Now, imagine that the daily hours of operation for your organization are longer than any one person's typical work day, the level and pace of when people need care is fluid and there is always a backlog of people waiting for help. And to add to it your boss said, "We're pretty flexible with when you work — just get your work done and make sure people get what they need." How might this go for someone? Especially for someone who cares deeply for the mission and is reluctant to set boundaries?

I'll tell you, and so could any other healthcare professional, pastor, teacher, YMCA staff member, social worker. It is intoxicating at first. Truly helping people brings a feeling of joy like no other. You quickly learn the work never stops, but the expectations and needs always increase. Over the next 6–12 months you begin to neglect personal care like working out or eating healthy, nothing too bad. Plus you're so busy at work you don't have time and are "working it off" anyway. Then, you begin to neglect your spirituality and your family. Your friends and social life take a back seat to the mission your heart bleeds for. All of a sudden, you believe you can't take a vacation and feel guilty being sick because someone may need something while you're out. All while your personal martyrdom for the mission becomes too much, you burnout, and within five years you quit altogether. It's likely you didn't have to strain too hard to imagine, whether you work in a nonprofit or not, this is the reality of work for many of us — especially for leaders.

We need boundaries to separate before we can really connect and commit to a cause, another person, and even to ourselves. They establish who we are and allow others to experience us as ourselves and meet your needs. We must learn to be independent before we can be dependent on others, and have them depend on us. Boundaries clarify personal priorities, values, thoughts, and feelings that are necessary to know, and be known by others, to deliver consistently on them over time and be known for having integrity. And yes, boundaries bring up discussions and disagreements that, while uncomfortable, are necessary for empowering and growing others, discovering personal and professional limits, and making good wise decisions over time. Setting boundaries doesn't mean you don't care. It means you care deeply about what is needed, what is important, and do the hard work of establishing the support and structure needed to lead and serve for the long-haul.

ACCEPT THE GOOD AND EMBRACE THE BAD

"It was nothing." But really it took a Herculean effort. "Nope, I don't want to know." When really you need to know you just don't want to embrace what's about to happen. Accepting the good and embracing the bad is a challenge. Especially for the humble, servant hearted, never gonna let you get me down optimistic servant leader. If I accept the good I might be seen as self-seeking or if I acknowledge the pain and problems I might be overwhelmed or be viewed as not believing enough. Neither are true. The integration of good and bad are needed to actually enjoy the good in life, grieve and grow through trials, and actually make positive change. A distorted view of reality will lead to a distorted view of what's needed. As leaders, accepting the good and embracing the bad is crucial to strong Character as often we must reconcile, in the same moment, the good and the bad. The needs of people and performance of the business. The struggles and limitations we face today and the vision we have for a brighter future. It is through the integration of the good and the bad that we build influence, demonstrate integrity, and ultimately deliver the Needed Service that creates tremendous impact in our lives and the lives of others.

On any given day as a leader you will need to embrace negative realities, celebrate wins, look at what's *still* needed to achieve the goal, receive a compliment for yesterday's success, receive difficult feedback on a mess up from the week before last, and strategize how to grow market share where there is no clear right or wrong answer, but maybe a good, better, best approach. Successful leaders are constantly clinging to what's possible, addressing issues, and celebrating the good that is happening. Internalizing what's really going on, good and bad, is necessary for progress. Without this ability, we are stuck with it being all good or all bad all the time. Perfection or debacle. And switching rapidly between them won't cut it. Switching, even if quickly, between all good and all bad results in whiplash — mentally and emotionally — for all involved — especially you. Leading others toward a shared purpose requires us to embrace the facts, to acknowledge and celebrate progress, to see the good in people while helping them to grow beyond where they are today.

How many of us want to offer better perks, pay, and benefits to team members? I hope all our hands are up. That is a good thing. And, you may not be where you'd like to be because of tight margins, down profitability, the cost of the benefit you'd like to offer, the size of the team, or the size of the organization. For some things, many things, this is my current reality. I am a huge believer in maternity and paternity time. I've taken leave for each of my three children. Twice paid, once unpaid. I want my team to have paid maternity and paternity. At the time of writing this book, we do not have the capacity to give paid leave. That frustrates me. Where I might be tempted to feel judged — there is no judgment. It is what it is. Where I could avoid it and say, "Eh, I don't even *have* to do this by law so why try or even think about it" — I do not. I accept that we want to offer this, and are generous with what we can do. I accept the reality of a small growing business, and strive to achieve that paid maternity/fraternity goal some day. Accepting the good and embracing the bad is needed with every strategic plan, annual goal, or personal development plan. Where is this realistic relentless optimism needed in your life, leadership, business?

This integration of good and bad is what produces resilient, secure, agile leaders who expect the most, and embrace whomever or whatever with compassion and an orientation toward growth and improvement. This is the Character that produces leaders who demonstrate integrity in the worst and the best of times.

EMOTIONAL AND POSITIONAL MATURITY

"I could never say that to them, they're my boss." Have you ever heard that? Said that? How about, "Who am I to tell them what to do?" Or maybe you or a coworker said, "Why am I getting blamed for this, it was James who said we should…" Emotional and positional maturity are required to lead with influence, and use your authority responsibly to serve — regardless of where you are, people you're with, or the position you hold. Emotional and positional maturity means you own who and how you are and have the ability to engage with others as equals. This results in personal confidence and competence with a respectful and respectable approach to authority and relationships.

The year was 2013. I was (am) a fanboy of Jon Acuff. I mean, what a great first name. The tour for his book *Start* brought him to the Mardel in Katy, Texas where I was going to meet him and we were going to become fast friends. Meghan was kind enough to go with me. We waited in line for 30 minutes. Now, it's my turn. I'm extroverted. Relatable. Adaptable. A charming conversationalist. This will be great. And it was. For Meghan. She and Jon had a fine conversation. Me on the other hand. I said SIX words — *Hey. Jon. Yes. Thanks so much.* This was supposed to be my moment to share the business I wanted to start, how much I appreciated Jon Acuff's witty, helpful commentary, and become friends which would eventually lead to a speaking tour headlined by Jon and Jon. Instead it exposed my emotional and positional *immaturity*. I realized this wasn't a "Jon Acuff is a celebrity" issue for me. It was with people in authority positions — bosses, CEOs, politicians, elders. If there was a real or perceived positional or status distance — I shrunk. I would lose my confidence. It was a struggle to engage in conflict, disagree, or share my opinion unless I knew it would please that person. And any potentially negative response or feedback from a person of authority would lead to an internal emotional spiral. A low-pressure book signing punctuated my inability to show up and lead in high-pressure situations.

When a healthy respect gives way to a you-must-be-holier-than-thou view of someone you erase any possibility of a healthy relationship. In that scenario the "authority" person must always approve, initiate, be right, and have all the answers. Your skewed perspective means you expect perfection from them. You will wither and place yourself as "less than" and move from servant to subservient in these hierarchy-based relationships. And since you don't have authority in this relationship you will seek to establish your own authority elsewhere — cascading an unhealthy hierarchical need for authority with others in your life. And this will further a mentality that various people or positions have a different worth or value. Unless you change the cycle, the cycle will continue.

In 2014, Jon Acuff spoke at the Sent conference. I knew what I needed to do. I'd already begun work on my emotional and positional maturity. I needed to take a step, albeit small, to overcome the hurdle in my mind. Jon finished his speech and sat down front and center. I made my way toward him weaving through tables. I pulled up a chair, sat next to him, stretched out my arm for a good handshake, and proceeded to tell him the whole story. After brief pleasantries he thanked me for coming over and sharing the story — and now we vacation together in Vermont. That's a joke. We don't vacation together and I cannot yet call him a friend. But, it was proof of what was possible. And this experience punctuated my ability to engage with another using emotional and positional maturity, regardless of status, position, and fame.

When you embrace and own your emotions, authority, and influence their control over you, and others control over you diminish. The very emotions and authority that controlled you become a strength and a tool to engage wherever, whenever, and with whomever needed. Emotions and position become ways to connect, serve, and influence not distance, direct or manipulate others. You gain the ability to traverse through social settings humbly, respectfully, and assertively if needed. You can manage your emotions and use them to relate well with others, receive hard truths, and show compassion. Owning emotions and engaging as equals precedes the ability to exercise leadership authority and empowering others to do the same. This Character aspect is the piece of the puzzle that allows you to humbly and confidently lead a mission larger than yourself and the key to unlocking a healthy relationship with yourself and others.

RELATIONSHIPS

I said earlier that one of the potential flaws of Character without Relationships is self-righteousness. Another is that if leaders create distance, they start to get a vague, opaque view of themselves. Usually, that view is based on stereotypes of what a leader "should be." Those *shoulds* include that leaders are to be isolated. Isolated because leaders take to heart the idea that "it's lonely at the top." Well really, leaders take that saying to heart, but thinking it means they don't get to have relationships.

The point is not to distrust everyone, but to realize you are in a unique position. You've probably tested this a time or two, whether it's with someone inside of the organization or somebody outside of the organization. You ask yourself, "Can I go to this person with this piece of information or with this potential shortcoming that I have, with this need, that I am looking to have filled?" Sometimes the person blows the trust or does not hold the information close. They're dismissive, or it wasn't someone who could give you what you needed, because of the positional relationship, or because they just didn't have that to give. Sometimes it's an easy miss, but sometimes it's a big one where, maybe, you shared a piece of information around somebody's future termination, or around future plans of the business and all of a sudden, it starts the tailspin of gossip. This leaves you feeling like you can't be transparent, vulnerable, that you have to shoulder all the weight alone, that you have to be the one to do the cheerleading or support. You think, "I always have to be on and be Jon the leader not Jon the person." Those false ideas, false starts, and false perceptions of Relationships are detrimental to our leadership.

It is the complete and total opposite that is true. In a 25-year Harvard study, David McClelland found that people form reference groups based on their shared values and aspirations, and that these groups have a significant impact on their motivation, goals, and success in life. People are more likely to be successful when they are surrounded by positive and supportive reference groups. So, you need to spend time with people, and the right ones. That also tells me that if you show me a leader without any friends, you'll find a scared, underachieving person who is at their wit's end. Because in isolation, depression goes up, anxiety goes up, stress goes up. We become distant from people and we start to disconnect. We don't have empathy. We don't think we can trust or rely on people. Conversely, if you look at the benefits of Relationships, healthy relationships lower anxiety and depression, they decrease isolation by definition, and they increase empathy.[13]

I think about your organization, your team, and their health. What are people struggling with most? People are super anxious and they're not engaged at work. They're getting burned out. They lack confidence in their abilities or their place in the organization. We do not give people the benefit of the doubt and we don't connect with empathy. There's often judgment and we continuously try to figure out how to build trust and be more collaborative. For all of these issues, and probably many more I did not list, the answer is relationship and connection with people. Relationships improve our mental health and our physical health. Stronger Relationships lead to more resilient, healthy, confident people who create even greater business results.

Going back to that Jenga analogy, if you end up with only one little block standing in between everything below and everything above, then Relationships are the piece that you want to leave standing in there. Because Relationships allow people to understand your Character and Relationships are needed to build Skills. It's the glue that binds us and keeps us from being either a distant executive or a know-it-all self-righteous, my way or the highway leader. So while there is no doubt all of us have been burned by relationships, even those failures are essential to the growth process.

Those failures also help us learn to find Relationships that can serve us, that can grow us, that allow us to be there for somebody, and that allow somebody to be there for us. They point us the truth that we need Relationships where we can speak the truth, where we can give (and get) encouragement, and where we can call people to act.

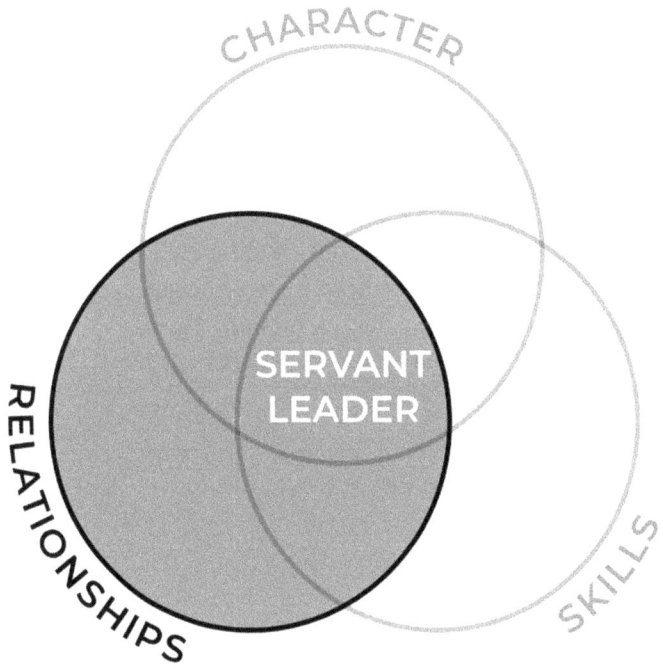

FIVE ASPECTS OF HEALTHY RELATIONSHIPS

Not all relationships are created equal. We have connections, acquaintances, and varying degrees of closeness with colleagues. However, all leaders need Relationships that fulfill our very specific needs. Dr. John Townsend says, "[...] *few people know about the potential of relating to others in ways that transform us, give us energy, and help us succeed.*" He outlines the relational needs, what he calls nutrients, each of us have, and the types of people we need in our life. (For more on this, check out his book *People Fuel.*)[14] This has influenced how I see relationships and teach leaders about the Relationships they need. I now believe that the following five aspects of Relationships are precursors for healthy leadership, and are what we need to give and receive from the people we are in Relationships with to be supported and be at our best.

Win-Win

Healthy Relationships are mutually beneficial. The best Relationships you have, your best friend, your spouse, your great family members, (not the cuckoo ones that you wish were gone), they want you to win. And you want them to win, too. They're a win-win. Relationships where we don't want the other person to win are potentially manipulative relationships. If I'm just using you for the things that I want and it's not a two-way street, if there is not both give and take, that is a problem. This mutually beneficial relationship means we can give and receive. It means we show up for celebrations, we act in the interests of others, and we strive to bring the next four attributes into our Relationships because we know it is good for each of us.

Presence

Being present doesn't just mean being in proximity to people. We've all been in the same room with someone and been light years away. The attribute of being present means you are present physically, yes, but also you are *present* — mentally and emotionally. When someone is present they are actively paying attention to others, the situation, and connecting emotionally. It is evident when there isn't an attempt to judge, fix or change the situation, just to understand what's going on and how you might be feeling. Presence with and from other people is needed in Relationships to build a strong connection and gives us the ability to give and receive what's needed throughout life.

Encouragement

All of us are uniquely talented in the various relational attributes. Maybe yours is truth-telling, or active listening and being present. Personally, and with many servant leaders I work with, encouragement is natural. So, time to shine my friends. Give that encouragement — we all need it. If an encouraging thought comes into your mind, make sure it comes out of your mouth. No one benefits if it stays in your head. Healthy Relationships are full of encouragement. Whether it is cheering on toward a goal, helping pick someone up after a mistake, or the pep talk before a big presentation encouragement gives us courage, energy, and belief in ourselves. Forgiving someone and releasing them from a hurt they caused, is a form of encouragement too. It reminds us that failure isn't final. The challenge for all of us, especially servant leaders, is to truly accept the good and the encouragement from others and fully internalize it. We need it for growth and to continue to go and do the work in front of us.

Truth

People in healthy Relationships tell each other the truth because we want them to win, care about them, and want the truth ourselves. The good, the bad, and the ugly. Unhealthy and artificial relationships tell people what they want to hear to keep up appearances, or keep the peace. Think about your friends and family who do speak the truth. The ones who say things like "No disrespect but" are typically tuned out and written off before too long. You likely appreciate it most from those who do it kindly, directly, and in a way that you know they are telling you because they really care. Speaking truth is a wonderful gift. The honest opinions, perspective, and insights from others are the foundation for a mutually beneficial relationship and for any and all personal growth. With the truth of others, we are destined to continue operating exactly like we do today.

Action

People in healthy Relationships will also call one another to act. And, they are uniquely qualified to influence one another because of the connection, honesty, encouragement, and foundation of mutual benefit they've built. Your best friends can say to you, "Hey, you said you were going to spend more time with the family and wanted me to help you hold to that ideal. What's going on? Go do it." People in healthy Relationships call each other up to be the best version of themselves. It is love for one another, and the desire to see the other person succeed that leads people to call people to act in their best interest emotionally, relationally, spiritually, professionally — you name it. We all get stuck. We all need accountability. We all need friends, and need to be the friend, who will call one another up to be the best we can be, to take action.

FIVE PEOPLE YOU NEED ON YOUR PERSONAL LEADERSHIP TEAM

We all need healthy Relationships to live, grow, and lead well. As a leader, especially one who is committed to serving, there are specific Relationships you need to lead at your best. You've probably heard "It's lonely at the top." Too often we confuse the reality of it being lonely with the idea that it has to be lonely. It's not true. And because it is often lonely it is even more important to find and nurture healthy Relationships. That's right, Relationships. Because the responsibility of leadership is heavy and potentially isolating, leaders need a team. A personal leadership team that will reinforce our Character and help us build our Skills to lead with even greater integrity, influence, and impact. The five types of Relationships you need on your personal leadership team are coach, mentor, cheerleader, friend, and partner. Without these Relationships we risk losing the balance needed to lead well. The balance of the mission, people, and performance. These five types of Relationships are what equip us, mature us, and give us what we need to receive to lead in the dynamic tension of serving and leading. Let's dive into the five Relationships you need on your personal leadership team and how to find someone to fill those roles.

Coach

Dr. John Townsend says in his book *People Fuel,* a coach is one who takes others down a path of growth and competency in a specific area.[14] I really like that definition. It's not just one area. We can have coaches in a bunch of different places in our lives. There are sports coaches, coaches for music, personal trainers are coaches, and at the time of writing this book I personally have a podcast coach and writing coach to help me improve in each of those areas. While we may need coaches for specific subjects, for your personal leadership team we are talking about a leadership or executive coach. A coach is someone who brings a structured approach to help you develop. A unique piece about a coaching relationship is it is a relationship where the coachee, you, gets to have it be all about you. Having a coach gives you an advocate whose focus is solely YOU — your goals, and what you need to get where you want to go.

I have had a leadership coach ever since I started leading. I've had an executive coach who helps me with my awareness, my emotional intelligence, and with my strategy. We can talk about my blind spots, we can set goals, have accountability, and I can report back on my successes and failures.

It is important to find a coach. You might be thinking, I've never had a coach, what should I look for in a leadership coach? There are coaches with a variety of certifications and specialties for various components of the business of leadership.

Look for a coach that specializes, is a subject matter expert, in whatever area you're trying to find in and grow in. For example, when I was an executive I had an executive coach. Now I have a podcast coach and I found someone who is an expert in writing books to coach me and work with me as I produced this book. In all these Relationships, there is a shared connection, and a balance of truth and grace that is oriented toward your growth.

A coach is going to have a structured approach, a framework, a definitive timetable or rhythm to what engagements look like. They are there not for their own growth, though that might happen, but to help you specifically meet your goals through a process they use. Coaching is a time where someone is specifically focused on you, what you need, and they know how to help you reach your goals. More often than not, there's going to be a very focused approach. There might even be advice, within boundaries. There is a guided or facilitated path to get you where you need to go.

They should also have good boundaries and there should be a structure. I am highly relational with all of my coaches. But there is also a healthy level of separation. Once you sign off the zoom, or you leave the room, I'm not assuming a coach is sitting there thinking about me. They may mull over something I said, but there is a time and a structure to our interactions that is clear and premeditated.

Mentor

One of the most common questions I get asked about your personal leadership team — Aren't a mentor and a coach basically the same thing? The answer — No. So, what's the difference between a coach and mentor? Three key differences are the intentionality, intensity, and the one-sidedness. A coaching relationship has a specific focus, structure, timeframe, and is much more of a one-sided relationship. Mentorship is more organic and fluid than a coaching relationship. It is often a mutually-beneficial Relationship where each person helps the others in a specific area. A mentor relationship can take many forms, but it is essentially an individual who is further ahead than you who you'd like to achieve what they've achieved, and do it like they did it. You're looking to spend time with, ask questions of, and learn from someone you admire who could become a trusted advisor.

How do you go about finding a mentor? First, you want to find someone you think you'd like to emulate. This could be a leader in your industry, a leader in your organization with a long track record of success, or someone you admire from networking or community groups. Once you've identified a few people it is important to figure out if you like each other. Merely walking up and saying, "I'd sure like to be like you one day, will you be my mentor" is probably not the best approach. Flattering, but not effective. Start by taking them to coffee or lunch. If there is a connection. Does this person have the time or interest? Do you get along and does the conversation flow pretty easily? Do you believe you can trust them? At this stage you're taking people to coffee, to lunch, and asking a bunch of questions to discover if they might be someone you could turn to for advice and learn from their experience.

Where the coach relationship is structured and rhythmic (biweekly, etc.), the mentor relationship can be more fluid and less frequent. Once a month, quarterly, or a conversation as needed may be what's needed and what each person can commit too. Here are a few examples from how I engage with my mentors, and from people we work with who have shared how they engage with a mentor:

→ Every other month calls with a retired CEO where you ask questions

→ Monthly coffee with a focus on 2–3 aspects of business, leadership, or life

→ Regular dinners with each other's families and calls as needed

→ Monthly group mentoring dinners or breakfasts where younger and older people seek to support and learn from each other — cross generationally

→ Ad hoc phone calls when issues arise and need advice

The key benefits of mentor Relationships are camaraderie, trusted advice, and the ability to learn from the success and failures of someone who has gone before you.

**Something to watch out for when mentoring is that it's not always a fit, especially in organizational mentoring programs. Often organizations try to prescribe mentors and mentees and it is rarely successful. I'm not talking about onboarding buddies, I'm talking about prescribing a leader who can guide another person. Pairing people often doesn't take into account the need for trust, admiration, and a mutual bond. And at worst, these types of programs turn us off to seeking a mentor because of the bad experiences. Organizations can help most by communicating the value of and need for a mentor, providing resources, tools, and checking to see that someone has a mentor, but let them identify and connect with the mentor themselves.

Cheerleader

Every leader needs a cheerleader. Why? Because you do hard work. It is stressful. Often demoralizing. You carry a tremendous responsibility for people and organizational success. The endless climb up the mountain to achieve the mission is daunting. And because you cheerlead a lot, serve a lot, and give a lot you need a cheerleader.

My wonderful wife is a great cheerleader of mine. The other day she turned to me and said, "I want you to know I'm so proud of you. I've never seen you work harder and more consistently than you are now. You work really hard. Then, you walk out and play hard with the kids, and spend time with me." Whoa — I was caught off guard. It was just what I needed that I didn't know I needed. I said, "Thank you, you don't know how much that means to me. I can go another six months on that statement alone! But you can keep telling me too."

To recharge the battery, fill the tank, and gain the confidence that comes from someone telling you that you can do it you need a person who will cheer you on. A cheerleader is someone who encourages you, reminds you all of the good things you are doing, someone who can tell you you're doing a good job, someone that motivates, inspires, and gives you the pep talk you need to keep fighting the good fight.

What should you look for in a cheerleader? They want you to win. They're going to be positive. Other people in your life, like friends, or coaches, or partners will reflect hard truths or tell you the unpleasant things you really need to hear — not your cheerleader. They may acknowledge you're down by ten and the odds are stacked against you, but they are also going to tell you that you can do it. A cheerleader is giving you the positivity, the encouragement, the hope you need to remain relentlessly optimistic and tirelessly committed to what's important to you in work and in life.

Friend

You need a non-work friend. You need work friends too, of course. It is much better to work with people you actually enjoy. But it's especially true that leaders need a friend (okay, friends — but let's start with one) outside of work. If you're going to lead and serve at your best, you need aspects of life where you're not leading or serving. You need a mutual relationship, where neither person is "in charge," where you enjoy each other, trust each other, want each other to win, and can engage in activities and discussions outside of a work context.

Here's why having a friend is so critical for leaders. Can we just call out how silly it is to have to point out friends are necessary — how far we've drifted from close friends and community that we're talking about this.

Anyway, a friendship, especially one outside of work, creates protection and accountability for leaders. Many times there isn't anyone you feel you can turn to. Or, you are the one ultimately in-charge of the business and don't have outside accountability. Maybe not even any accountability. A friend is someone you can confide in if you really mess up, go to if you need help, and who can call you to do better. Another specific benefit of a close friendship, a mutually beneficial one is it teaches each of us to give and to receive. As a servant leader, you're a generous giver. Many times all you do is give, give, give. You need to receive. A friendship helps train that muscle. When you can learn to give and receive freely it permeates your spirit and influences your ability to give even more, to ask for what you need or what the business needs.

A friend, a true friend, the kind that is closer than a brother or a sister, comes from a friendship with commitment — even through struggles and mistakes, that is fun, where you can completely be yourself, and where no one is really in-charge but you want the best for each other and help each other be their best. Great, but how do we find this person as an adult, right? If we were kids we'd just walk up to someone at lunch who dresses like us and announce we're best friends. It's so much harder for adults. You may already have this friend, you might simply need to lean into building the Relationship. Start by focusing on the attributes of a healthy Relationship. If you don't think you have anyone, start with places where people are doing things you enjoy, with shared values like a volunteer group, a gym, a church, art or music festivals. Put yourself out there, be patient, and be the friend you want to have and you will likely create the friendship you are seeking.

Partner

We said earlier — it's lonely at the top. Even more reason to take someone with you and partner up to do this work together. The fifth Relationship every leader needs on their personal leadership team is a partner. This is the only person on your personal leadership team that must work with you. Same place of employment. This is not a business partner or a life partner, though it can sometimes be either of those. I am talking about a colleague who you can co-labor with who complements you. A good partner is trustworthy, aligned on values, and shares your vision or goals. They are your right-hand person who often can challenge you like others won't, has strengths to compliment your weaknesses, and who often thinks differently than you do. There is no duplication here. Your partner should not be your clone.

Think about it. You see this in many workplaces. An entrepreneur gifted in sales will work with someone better at operations. A CEO will bring "their person" when they switch organizations. You naturally gravitate toward someone on your team who advises you, takes work from you, or tells you behind closed doors what you really need to hear. Because of the stress, the pressure, the workload we will naturally look for these partners. Now that you're aware, be intentional in finding this person, cultivating the trust needed, and outlining specifically how each of you can complement the other and grow each other beyond where either of you could go on your own.

It is through the Relationships we have and create that we are able to live, grow, and lead at our best. People are not meant to go it alone, and leadership is not a solo-endeavor.

In the margin of this book, or in a notebook, write coach, mentor, friend, cheerleader, and partner. Now, write someone's name next to each word. Even if they are not yet your coach, mentor, friend, cheerleader, or partner — write it down. **Now, use the people who are already in these roles for you. Go ask the people you wrote down that could be that person. Go find someone if you left that role blank.**

Focus on cultivating healthy Relationships and building your personal leadership team to create the support you need to succeed, the connection you need to refine your Character, and the growth that will lead to even greater impact where you lead and with the people you serve.

SKILLS

To go back to the Jenga blocks, the third thing we need in our scaffold is Skills. Without defined Skills, if all you have is Character, you can have a high moral standard, but not know in any practical way what to do. If all you have are Relationships, you may be a great person who can't deliver on what you say you will and this will fail to advance the mission of your organization. Both of these situations limit your impact in the world. Without skills, there is no way to influence, no way to create and steward any impact. Skills are where the rubber meets the road, if you will. Skills take the influence we've earned through Relationships and the integrity produced by our Character and turn them into impact.

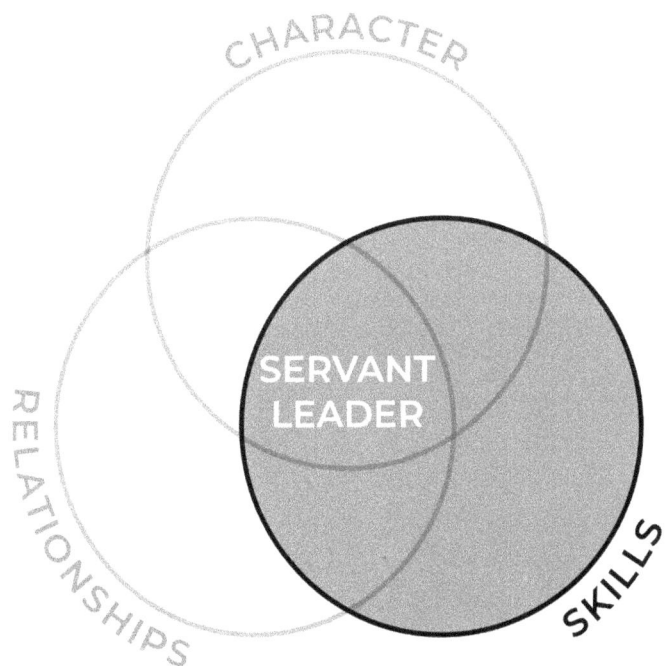

There are eight essential Skills we are going to address in this book. All eight could be a book on their own. When I work with clients and organizations we spend a long time working on these Skills. We teach and learn and practice. I encourage you to skim each Skill. Yep, you heard me. They will always be here. Use this book as a reference, especially when you feel you need to grow in one of these Skills, but it is also a lot. Leaders need to be competent in a variety of Skills. I am introducing them here so that you can think about how you, your team and your organization might work toward more impact and stronger servant leadership. The Skills are: service, expertise, vision casting, emotional intelligence, communication, discernment, development, and activation. I will number them, not because of priority or a required sequence (although the sequence helps), but to help guide you through them.

I am not attempting, in the slightest, to create an exhaustive list of leadership skills. Is that even possible? We will introduce Skills that are fundamental, foundational even for each of us as leaders to effectively lead and serve. I will ask some questions to ponder for each skill. This is a way of starting the learning process for that skill — knowing it could go on for a lifetime or need support from a coach.

Skill #1 — Service

The first Skill, the central Skill, is actually to serve. If you are wondering, is that a Skill? I would say it is because to serve or service is the very action performed for the benefit of the object. We said before that love is an act of the will, for the benefit of the object, followed by an emotion. Service is that action performed. In my mind, love and service are synonymous. Where true service exists, there will be love. Where true love exists, there must be service. How many of us say, "I love what I do?" I hope we all can. And, when we do — we express that through serving.

Serving is at the core of a leader's Skills. Even when we are imperfect, if we are skillful at serving it allows us to stay mission driven, to stay focused on our people, and to really balance people and the performance needed to deliver results. If you start from a place of service, and that is the primary motivator, it will keep the heart in touch with why you do the work. Serving is central and with a heart to serve — to benefit what and who we serve — we can hold the tension of difficult choices that may be painful in the now, but produce better results in the future. Truly serving means I can and will act for the benefit of something outside of myself.

So what does that look like for a leader?

We serve three priorities as servant leaders:
1. **We serve the mission. I lead with the mission in mind**
2. **We serve the people. I act for the benefit of others.**
3. **We serve to deliver results. I strive to achieve the goal for the benefits produced for all involved.**

What are some questions that help us serve those priorities?

→ What's the purpose?

→ Who is it for?

→ What does success look like?

Just answering those questions will help change organizational culture, creating more clarity. If everything we did, every decision we made had to run through those questions we would be more impactful leaders overnight. We'd make better decisions in difficult scenarios, we would communicate better, we would make better policies, and set better expectations. The answers to these questions also give us a map to which Skills to use to best serve in the various situations we encounter. Let's jump into some of the more concrete specific Skills that leaders need to be able to do that.

Skill #2 — Expertise

You have to show up with some sort of competence when you are a servant leader. I don't mean you have to be an IT expert to lead IT, and you do not have to be a marketing expert to lead marketing. Expertise is no doubt beneficial and often most effective, but not a requirement for leading functional business areas. What your expertise is, is the talent you have plus the competence you've developed around that talent. Having a track record of demonstrated competence, and success, in a specific skill, area, or industry is the critical component, beyond Relationships, that establishes your credibility, reputation, and enables your ability to uniquely serve a situation.

Because of your expertise, you're likely able to operate faster. On top of that, you produce better results with less effort and connect the dots for how your area interacts with other parts of the team or organization. You can contextualize the value, need, and place it fits. This allows you to serve the highest level need with the talent you have. When you can serve from your expertise, you will invite others to serve from theirs. Beyond bringing competence, knowing and operating from your expertise invites collaboration because you can value others expertise as well. You can confidently say "I don't know," ask questions, and invite others to contribute because you are sure of the area you do know, answer questions, and contribute to goals. Foster your expertise to serve even greater in specific areas, and help others foster theirs. Imagine what's possible when a service-oriented team of experts work to solve big, hairy problems — together.

What are a few (not in any way a complete list of) areas of expertise? Sales, finance, marketing, communications, teaching, public speaking, writing code, manual labor, organizing people, planning, and analyzing data or situations. We could go on.

What are some questions to help you hone in on your specific expertise?

→ What comes more naturally to you than it does to others, that you enjoy, and that others tell you that you do well?

→ What aspect of work or leadership do you excel at and continue to work to develop?

→ Where do you have a track record of success?

With a heart and Skill to serve, plus your expertise, you will make a tremendous difference for your team, your work, your community — there is no doubt. We've also said that leaders influence others toward a shared purpose. Which makes our next Skill a critical one.

Skill #3 — Vision Casting

You may have heard the proverb, "Where there is no vision, the people perish." Well, perishing certainly doesn't serve. A critical Skill for servant leaders is vision casting. Clearly communicating what's needed, the bright, better desired future that will direct, inspire, and unite. It gives inspiration. It connects a person's day-to-day work with the impact of that work. A vision aligns and focuses the efforts to meet the purpose, or mission, of your organization. Great visions are profitable — meaning they benefit the purpose, the people, and the bottom line of the organization.

At Leadwell, we get the privilege of working with lots of nonprofits. This means there is a board and stakeholders, and they operate as a non-profit because their work is for "a societal benefit." We often get asked, "How does a leader even go about getting that vision? Is it my job to cast the vision? Do we do it as a group? Is it what people tell us they want or what we see might be needed?" Listen, most of us have been in a room with 40 different people who have 40 different ideas about the direction that's needed.

Regardless of an organization's tax status, a sole proprietorship, or a community group, a vision that is created in isolation will likely fail. It is the leader's responsibility to make sure a vision is set and to cast the vision. Without a leader who holds the Skill of vision casting, things will never take off or fall apart. It doesn't mean they must do it alone. Great visions are created in conversation, with input from numerous sources, from shared experiences, and the expression of what each believes is needed. Like a funnel it starts wide and narrows in based on needs, goals, opportunities, strengths, the marketplace, and the resources available. Leaders do not have to set the vision alone, but they are responsible to ensure it is set.

Here are some questions to consider when setting the vision:

→   What problem breaks your heart that you are called to address?

→   Where can our organization be the best and make the biggest impact?

→   What is needed now to make what may be needed next possible?

Once you've worked through the process here is a formula for writing a vision. *What were we going to achieve by when and why is it important.* That is the Skill of vision casting in one sentence — if you can do that, you can cast a vision that clearly communicates what's needed so you can direct, inspire, and unite your service-oriented team.

We will achieve _____ *by* _____
because _____.

Now that the vision is set, it needs to be communicated. We are going to come back to communication. These Skills are not exactly sequential. Serve→ Expertise→ Vision Casting→ Emotional Intelligence→ Communication→ Development→ Discernment→ Activation. However, they do work well in a sequence, like I said when I introduced the Skills portion of this book. It sure is hard to activate someone without a vision — for a small project or to address a world-changing problem. So, because emotional intelligence is so critical to our communication, development, discernment, and activation of others — we go there next.

Skill #4 — Emotional Intelligence

The next Skill a leader needs to work on to be able to serve and influence is emotional intelligence. Most folks will either nod and say "Yes I know that," or will sigh and write it off because they believe you either have it or you don't. However, consider how you reacted the first time you lost a client or delivered a performance review, and how you react to those things now. Different or the same? Have you matured?

I hope we can make it really practical because emotional intelligence is the connective tissue between all the other Skills. Emotional Intelligence is potentially the most valuable Skill a leader has because it is about yourself first and then other people. And it sure is challenging to influence others if we can't influence ourselves while understanding what's going on with others — and what they or a situation may need.

Daniel Goleman, the godfather of emotional intelligence, or EQ, describes this Skill as understanding and managing your own emotions and influencing the emotions of others. He talks about five specific areas of emotional intelligence. Empathy, social skills, self awareness, motivation, and self regulation. Because some are/have been addressed elsewhere (motivation — activation, empathy and social skills — Relationships and communication) and for the sake of this book we will focus on three areas and call them self awareness, others awareness, and regulation.[15]

Self-Awareness

Self-awareness is your ability to perceive and understand the things going on in you and make you who you are — your personality, beliefs, values, feelings, thoughts, and actions. Where it may be uncomfortable to focus on yourself, especially for an others-oriented servant leader, it is critical to know yourself and what's going on so that you can help others, yes, and also operate in integrity and respond to others and the situation in a way that best serves everyone involved. Without self-awareness you limit your ability to empathize, to connect, to feel. Self-awareness precedes self-leadership. So, how can you lead yourself as you intend and grow your self-awareness?

We become more self-aware the more clearly we see and know ourselves as we truly are. One way is through something we've already discussed: Relationships. Having a coach, a mentor, a friend, a partner, and a cheerleader will help us to learn about ourselves, our values, and feelings. These folks, our closest circle, can act as a mirror for us showing how we come across and how we might be behaving in specific situations. Because of the relationship, they can provide feedback.

Feedback is another powerful way to grow self awareness, especially when combined with self-reflection. The practice of reflection or journaling are great tools to formulate and articulate what you are learning about yourself. Skills or personality assessments are also helpful tools. These are plentiful and they all help us gain information about ourselves. *I caution you to use them to identify patterns and paint a clear picture of you — not box you in to who and how you must be.* These assessments can be useful for looking at communication, your strengths, creativity, or how you react to stress.

Self-awareness is critical to leading ourselves and others, to knowing what's important to you, your priorities, your tendencies, how you might make decisions, how you feel about certain things, and what triggers you. It is most helpful when you operate out of this understanding and in the moment can personally assess… How am I _____? In these moments, ask yourself, how am I feeling? Thinking. Acting. This personal insight opens your ability to gain insight about others and respond accordingly.

Others-Awareness

If we do not pause and be present we will never be truly aware of what's going on around us, especially what's going on with people around us. So much of what is actually going on with people is unseen. If self-awareness is your ability to perceive and understand yourself, others-awareness is your ability to perceive and understand others, demonstrated through your acknowledgment and response.

How do we grow our others-awareness? The first step towards others-awareness is making the time and giving the attention needed to be present. That is both a physical *be present* and a mental and emotional presence, too.

I am not too proud to say that there have been plenty of times in my life where I might be sitting at the dinner table with my family, or on the couch with Meghan, and I'm physically there but I'm also 1000 miles away. If I don't actively work to be present, I can't really show up. I work on presence in a few ways. I make lists so things are not hanging out in my mind bugging me. I have learned to come back to focus in the present by having a pause practice. I learn and grow by taking feedback from my inner circle. I do all this because I know that I won't be able to empathize or identify with or even have enough information to sincerely comfort somebody if I am not there. Or, honestly, I won't even have the insight to tell somebody something difficult that they need to hear and call them to act if I am mentally and emotionally somewhere else.

Being others-aware gives us the ability and the opportunity to feel with folks and to focus on connecting with them. Once present, you can empathize by giving someone the connection they need. You can take the time to be curious, to pay attention to non-verbal cues, and to respond with wisdom, truth, or encouragement. Being others-aware gives you the insight to know whether or not to solve a problem, sit in a problem with someone, or offer the support they need to solve it themselves. If we are not aware of what anyone is thinking, feeling, or doing, then we have no opportunity to, as Goldman says, influence the emotions of others. Without the others-awareness, we limit our ability to influence people.

Regulation

Regulation is the application of all of the above, often in what feels like really challenging circumstances. It could be sitting with someone who lost a loved one or having a courageous conversation about a team members' performance when they flip it and accuse you, and you need to respond well in these emotional situations. Our ability to regulate is the outward expression of the internal Character work we discussed earlier (emotional maturity, boundaries, embracing the bad, maintaining relationships). It is how we show we have the ability to meet the demands of reality, and do so in a way that is helpful and appropriate — for us, others, and the situation.

That's a lot. Let's take a…

…pause…

Learning to take that pause helps with regulation. It separates stimulus and response and gives your brain time to process (or catch up with) what is going on. From a short 3–5 second pause, to a quick breathing exercise, or even waiting to send that email for 24 hours — the pause is a practice that allows you to respond using all the tools you've practiced.

Beyond pausing, there are numerous techniques to help with regulation. Using our question "How am I _____?" in the moment helps identify feelings, thoughts, and behaviors. Other questions like, "Is this true?" help accurately assess what's going on. Being well rested and having the type of Relationship where you can vocalize what you're internally processing are all helpful. And, sometimes what's going on is so heavy you need to do more than work it out in your head.

March 12, 2020 was heavy. COVID. Furloughs, layoffs, lost funding, being locked in the house, my wife pregnant with kiddo number two, and more was weighing on me. I never had a panic attack, and only ever felt mild anxiety, but I could feel this. I felt it in my chest, I would shake occasionally, could not focus, could not complete my regular morning run, and felt sick. The second week of COVID I couldn't fill my lungs. I would breathe, full breaths, but never felt satisfied. Shortly thereafter I collapsed to my knees in front of my blue chair crying uncontrollably. I was unsuccessfully trying to fill my lungs. I remember saying, "I can't do it."

The weight on my shoulders was too heavy to bear. I began grabbing at my shoulders and pulling things off. I began to focus on laying things down. I kept saying, "I can't do it," and prayerfully grabbing things off my shoulders, my back, carrying them forward with two hands and laying them down. I began to name them as I pulled them off and laid them down. I began to breathe again. By the grace of God, the anxiety, stress, and breathing issues were lifted. I discovered a powerful regulation tool in making the intangible tangible and physically moving it from where I was feeling it to another place entirely. To a place where it could be managed. When needed, I still use this practice today.

Here are three questions to ask yourself — in private, in the moment, as needed to help you lead and serve with emotional intelligence:

→ How am I _____? (feeling, thinking, acting, etc.)

→ How might they be _____? (feeling, thinking, experiencing, acting, etc.)

→ What is required of me right now?

We introduced emotional intelligence prior to communication because our ability to know ourselves, read and respond to others and the situation, and also to be able to regulate our emotions are critical to communicating and communicating well.

Skill #5 — Communication

I wonder how many times I can say "this is likely the most critical Skill for a leader?" I've said it for vision casting. I've said it for emotional intelligence. I will say it again for communication. This really might be the most critical Skill, until we get to discernment, then discernment will be the most critical Skill. ;)

As leaders, If we go overboard in any one area, it should be communication. The goal of a leader should be to over communicate to the point of nausea. Let's level-set quickly about the Skill of Communication. There are books upon books about communication. We won't cover everything here. How could we? We will focus on three critical components of communicating well as leaders.

As a leader, everything speaks. Everything said, not said, done, not done is being interpreted as you communicating something. Often that is true, not always. And the sooner we learn that as leaders everything we do communicates something, everything speaks, the better.

The great news is that communication isn't just from you going out. Communication is also a two-way street. It is an in and it's an out. Let's dive into the three components of communication that leaders need to do this well. They are equally important, and often best done in sequence: listen, understand, and share.

Listen

Focus on absorbing all that is being shared, verbal and nonverbal. From all that is communicated less than 30% is verbal. Some say only 7% is verbal. So, listen with your eyes, ears, and pay attention to tone. Listening is active. It requires that you quiet your mind so you can let what's being shared take priority in the moment. Listening requires circling back to our ability to regulate so that you can intentionally be present and suspend judgment. This means holding back your response or judgment of the situation, information, or individual. We can respond or make a judgment later. Separate the listening from the assessing and the responding to listen well and learn the most so you can communicate the best.

Understand

When you slow your response, you create space to connect — with the person and what's being said. You give yourself the opportunity to, as Covey said in *The 7 Habits of Highly Effective People,* "Seek first to understand, before being understood."[16] We immediately build perceptions and interpretations based on what we hear and see. Moving through those by curiously trying to clarify the intended message helps us understand more clearly. After listening, the key to gaining a clear understanding is to lean into your childlike curiosity. Kids ask significantly more questions each day than adults. If you've been around children, you know this is true. The result of their questions is 1 quadrillion synapses building bridges in between information, rationale, and explanation.[17] Kids are learning machines and questions are their super power to understand. The better our questions, the better our understanding. Start with simple, factual open-ended questions.

→   What does that mean?

→   How are you?

→   What do you think?

Then, ask the second question. This is the breakthrough where you clarify your perceptions and interpretations.

→ Why is that important for us today?

→ What makes today good?

→ What makes you think that?

If you truly want to master understanding, be bold enough to stay curious and ask questions until you discover what's truly going on. Then, reflect what you think you heard. You'll know you truly understand when they respond to your summary with, "You nailed it." "Exactly!" Or, "That's it."

In communication, you are responsible for making sure the message is delivered and received as intended. It is your responsibility to seek to understand, and your responsibility to speak and share, saying what you intend to say and what's needed.

Share

It is your responsibility to communicate so it is delivered and received as intended. It's said that we don't really internalize what we hear until we hear it 21 times. So, accept that leaders are repeaters and be prepared to share a lot. If it is worth saying, it is worth saying over and over and over again. Share the vision, expectations, values, needs, decisions, potentially misinterpreted information, you name it, you likely need to communicate it over and over and… you get it.

When the message is clear, concise, and compelling the message is understood, as simply and quickly as possible, in a way that inspires action. To make your message clear ask yourself:

"What do I want them to know/do?"

Invite others to review and give feedback on your message to help make what you're saying clear to others, not just you. And, say the same message in different ways, different mediums, and at different times.

One reason you say it over and over is because being concise means saying less at once, which naturally leads to needing to communicate more frequently. To aid in making your communication more concise, ask yourself:

"How can I say this in fewer words?"

Speak in the active voice and avoid unnecessary words. A CEO client of mine pointed out that the word *that* is completely unnecessary. You try. Go remove "that" and see if your sentence still makes sense. I did. Oftentimes, it did. While I don't agree ~~that~~ the word *that* is unnecessary, I do see his point. Avoid unnecessary words so *that* your message is more concise.

Finally, our message needs to be compelling so that it inspires action. As a leader we have the opportunity to connect all of the activities to why we do the work — from payroll, to HR, to keeping the lights on and the floor swept. All work is valuable and needed, sometimes we forget. And, sometimes we need to connect the dots on the importance of deadlines or of executing a project at a certain standard. To communicate in a more compelling way ask yourself:

"Why does this matter?"

When you do you gain the ability to connect action to inspiration and activate people to do great work.

We've asked a number of questions so far about communication. **Here are three to help you communicate in each of the three key components of communication — listening, understanding, and sharing:**

→ What is getting in the way of me listening, and what can I do about it?

→ What question might help me gain a better understanding?

→ How can I share this in a more clear, concise, and compelling way?

We've progressed through a majority of the Skills we will cover. That progress goes something like this: Have the emotional intelligence to be aware and respond appropriately so as to communicate well, allowing you to discern what is best. These Skills are complementary. Each one stands alone, but is strengthened by the others too. And, discernment requires pulling together a multitude of Skills, experiences, information, and people to make wise decisions.

Skill #6 — Discernment

What is discernment? Discernment isn't just having all the answers. Or the right answers. And, it isn't just doing all the right things. Discernment is the ability to perceive, understand, and make decisions clearly. Especially where it is not obvious. Like with tomatoes. Discernment might be summed up as: knowledge is knowing that a tomato is a fruit, discernment is knowing not to put it on a fruit salad. Discernment is the intersection of Skill, knowledge, and intuition that enables wise decisions and appropriate action.

When leaders use the Skill of discernment it appears as though they're playing with a few extra cards up their sleeves. And, you can tell when discernment is used by leaders to serve because the decisions and actions point to the mission, are fair, avoid stirring up conflict, but try to bring peace, are open to debate, not forced upon others, and produce results.

The biggest limitation of this Skill is not knowledge, resources, or experience. We, each of us, limit our own ability to make wise decisions and act on them through our pride or fear. The big "What if…" questions can throw us. A scarcity versus abundance mindset creates how we look at things. Our focus on avoiding discomfort, even if for a little while, fuels short-term fixes instead of long-term solutions. Profits. Processes. Policies. If we focus, and prioritize, avoiding what could go wrong instead of doing what is right, what best serves the mission and the people, we will make bad decisions.

Discerning between turkey or ham sandwich for lunch is low risk and has little impact. However, many of the situations you face as a leader do involve risk and have huge impacts on bottom lines and peoples' lives. Situations like direction changes of a project or organization. The difficult times when you must release a team member, stop delivering a product/service to people who do benefit, or God forbid, need to do "damage control" because of a crisis or major mistake. Navigating differences, doubling down on your convictions, or delaying opportunities are all especially challenging, and critical areas of discernment.

The decisions and actions in each of these require and reveal the Character and priorities of ourselves and our organizations. The scenarios require courage, humility, and assertiveness. The stronger your Character and Relationships, the better equipped you are to wisely navigate these critical areas of discernment to make sure the purpose, the people, and the place are served.

There are countless questions that aid in decision-making. Many have been listed amongst the other Skills. Better questions often lead to better answers, and when it comes to discernment, asking more and better questions, early and often is a recipe for success.

Here are three that help:

→   What other information, people, or experience will be helpful in making the best decision?

→   What results (positive or negative) might this decision create?

→   Does this create an opportunity to serve the mission and the people?

Skill #7 — Development

Why is development a required Skill? You might be thinking, "I don't work in fundraising or business development." The entire act of leadership and business is an act of development. It doesn't matter if you're starting a business, launching a project, if you are organizing people to go volunteer and plant trees, you are aiming to grow (develop) from what is to what could be. As a servant leader, developing people or relationships, developing projects or initiatives, developing organizations is critical to our role. As we aim to influence the attitudes, thoughts, and behaviors of others towards a shared purpose, we need to see the whole back half of the definition as being about development, and grow our own Skills to develop others.

The best place to start a business, project, working relationship, development plan… well, anything really… is where our definition of leadership ends. With *a shared purpose.* If you're trying to create a business partnership with someone who doesn't want a partnership, it won't go anywhere. The same is true with a donor, volunteer, or a team member.

One of the hardest parts of developing people is figuring out *where your support ends,*

and the work that *only they can do begins.*

The first step for all development is to identify the goal (why and what) and get clear on it so everyone can be on the same page.

Your role in developing others is critical, and you have two of them to play. One of your roles is to model the way, and the second is to support others' growth.

Development starts with leading by example. Being the growing, learning leader who has their own growth goals — personally and professionally. Exemplifying the expectation that growth is essential. Modeling the behaviors, rhythms, and practices that you want to see in others. Modeling the way is critical because your impact grows when you do. When you continually model what it is like to be a growing leader — you will grow. Modeling the way is also critical because more is caught than taught. People around you will learn and grow more from what you do, than what you say. However, that doesn't exclude the second part of your role in developing others — supporting their growth.

Your second role in developing others is supporting others' growth. Support will look different for different people. Some need encouragement. Some need challenges. Some people want to hear your stories and learn from your experiences, while others want specific, actionable feedback. The goal is not to be all things, it is to give what is needed for the individual to be able to achieve the target, the standard that is set. This often includes supporting with training, time to learn, stretch assignments or projects, coaching — from you or a professional coach. Show your support by making this a priority, for you and them, by giving what's needed, and by giving them the time and space it takes to learn and grow.

One of the hardest parts is often figuring out where support ends and the work that only they can do begins. The desire to help isn't helpful when the challenge is removed entirely. No matter how involved we were up to this point, it's time to get out of the way. You must, otherwise you will be refining your own Skills and abilities, not developing theirs. This is the part of the plan that we can't do ourselves. Give them the room to run and work their plan. Let them win. Let them make mistakes. Let them have the fun. They won't grow otherwise. You are the coach. You are the mentor. YOU are the leader. You are there, to help them, to support them, to challenge them, to ensure that the structure still exists and that they are moving forward.

As leaders, our role is to help set the target, model the way, support and empower our people, and give them the room to run and do the growth work.

Here are questions we can ask to help us guide the development process:

→ What growth is needed to achieve the desired future? (Ask yourself and the other person)

→ What does it look like for me to model the outcomes I desire to see?

→ How can I best equip this growth while giving space for the person to do what's needed?

Skill #8 — Activation

Development is a requirement in leadership, in business, in life. And so is activating people. We have to send people, we have to say "Go!" — we have to initiate action so we can actually set about doing these things we say and set out to do. Activating people to do work. Good, meaningful work is an act of service.

In the definition of servant leadership we talk about leadership as an act. Leadership is not a position or a title. It's an action. Leaders need to activate others towards a shared purpose, because if we don't move toward a shared purpose, there isn't growth. We can't influence others' thoughts, attitudes, or behaviors without activation. The first, and best, way to do this is by leading by example. One of the greatest strengths servant leaders have is we get in the trenches, hands dirty, move boxes, get sweaty, whatever it is that needs doing. We will model the way and inspire folks to do what they wouldn't otherwise do.

Then we need to invite others to get in there with us. You must say, "I need help, your help specifically, and here is what you can do…." We must continue to activate ourselves and others to achieve what otherwise would not be possible. You cannot do it alone, you probably don't want to, and you shouldn't — it is better to have more people involved. Because you know the benefit for everyone who is involved in doing good and meaningful work.

Your activation is an invitation for them to contribute in a way that only they can, with the Skills and the tools and the talents that you need, that they need, that the mission needs to be able to reach its full potential.

You must say both, "Go!," and, "I need your help." You must say, "Here's why we do X, Y and Z." You must invite others to contribute. And, yes, you must cast a vision. Yes, you must clarify goals. Yes, it's best to model the way. But you must, you must, you must also invite others to contribute. Activation begins with leading by example and ends with clearly inviting and asserting what is needed to succeed and to serve.

Here are three questions to ask yourself when you are thinking about activating an individual or a group with a clear, compelling call to action:

→ What needs to be done?

→ Why does it matter?

→ Who is best to help with this?

The reason I'm so adamant about the necessity of these Skills is that I know from personal experience, and working with thousands of leaders, that:

a) having the Skills needed to deliver on the vision and help others succeed builds a leader's credibility and influence.

b) these specific Skills allow servant leaders to live in the tension of what servant leadership really means.

For too long, I thought (and relied on) one attribute of servant leadership. My character. I reminded myself that character determined my capacity. True. However, I diminished my Character by downplaying the necessity of Relationships for my support and the Skills needed to deliver on commitments and drive impact. Without all three — Character, Relationships, and Skills — I had big holes in my Jenga tower. It kept falling down. I couldn't build it fast enough or hold it all together. And, without integrating all three attributes, it will be the same for you. Character calls us up. Relationships keep us from falling. Skills drive impactful results.

Just like we had to realign our idea of the attributes of servant leadership. Not Character, Relationships, *or* Skills. Character, Relationships, and Skills. We need to replace some myths that keep you from a) integrating those three attributes, b) embracing the tension of servant leadership, and c) amplifying your integrity, influence, and impact. In the next section, we are going to dive into ten myths that we need to replace about servant leadership. When you replace the myths with what's really needed for servant leadership you will grow your integrity, influence, and impact.

REPLACE

Your input determines your outlook.
Your outlook determines your output,
And your output determines your future.

— Zig Ziglar[18]

OUT WITH THE OLD, IN WITH WHAT'S TRUE

Have you ever overused a good thing? I know I have. The problem is that overusing a good thing leads to it becoming a bad thing — in our leadership, in many places in life, and I discovered this... with running shoes.

I am a runner. I have been a runner for fifteen years. I've also been getting older over those fifteen years. I run three miles most days of the week. About five years ago, I was running, like I have always done. After my run I realized that my leg was hurting. I don't remember doing anything to hurt it. So, I assumed it was because I was getting old. I didn't think too much of it. However, the slight discomfort turned into an annoyance that led to all out pain. Every day. Whether I ran or rested. I was at a loss. I am a runner. I must run. What do I need to do to keep running?

I began to research how to keep running as you get older. The internet told me about ALL the things I wasn't doing and needed to be doing. I need to hydrate more. I could no longer roll out of bed, eyes barely open, and stumble my way into a jog. I needed to warm up. The internet also told me about the importance of stretching. For the guy who cannot touch his toes unless all the boxes are checked; it is hot, I've already run, and you push my back while I grunt my way forward in pain — stretching sounded like a useful, and terrible, solution. The thing is, a couple of days had passed. I was in more pain than before so I was willing to try anything. I drank more water, warmed up (kind of), and began stretching after my run or later in the day. Still in pain. So, along with adding ibuprofen to the mix of solutions I enlisted my wife to help me stretch. More than the assist I needed to touch my toes, she added in the accountability I needed to do it. She also brought some wisdom the internet didn't provide.

In the middle of a hamstring stretch for my left leg Meghan asks me, "When was the last time you replaced your shoes?" My shoes? My shoes are great. I tell her very clearly it is not the shoes, it is that I am getting older. She's not convinced. She goes on to tell me, "You should replace your shoes every 400 miles or so and you're probably 4000 miles past that." Okay, that might be true — for other people. But I like my shoes, they are comfortable, and I am just getting old.

She was so sure this was the solution that she bought me new shoes. Reluctantly, I switched over to the new shoes. I ran for three days in those new shoes and then… my leg pain was gone. It was 100% gone. When I switched shoes I also dropped all the extras. The extra water, warm up, stretching, and after the first day or two ibuprofen as well. I had worn my shoes out. The real truth was I wore my shoes so far out that they went from being a good fit to a limiting factor on my running and overall health. I needed to replace my shoes to regain my ability to run, and live well, for the long run.

I realized that sometimes the solution isn't adding one more good thing to the mix. One more habit. Or, tinkering with what is overused or worn out and changing the process just a little bit, trying to take a tool (or leadership practice or style) that is meant to serve in a specific scenario and rely on it in every scenario or overuse it to the point of wearing out its effectiveness. Sometimes, we need to entirely replace what doesn't serve us anymore.

There are a lot of comfortable myths, misconceptions, and norms floating around servant leadership and how Servant Leaders must act. I know replacing the practices we're used to with principles and practices that are unknown is challenging. We ask ourselves, how do I know this will work? What will people think? Let me tell you that when you replace the untrue, worn out ideas surrounding servant leadership with principles and practices that truly serve, even though it is hard to switch, the result will be less pain, guilt, and frustration. Plus a newfound freedom to serve with your whole self and the ability to amplify your integrity, influence, and impact.

We already redefined servant leadership. We also walked through our need to realign around the three attributes leaders need, and how to lead with and through your Character, Relationships, and Skills. Now, we need to replace the myths, misconceptions, and norms we think we have to follow as Servant Leaders. We must replace them so that we, and the people we lead, may run.

ONE-DEGREE OFF AND WORLDS APART

I told you I used ibuprofen to help cover my leg pain for a season. The problem was what began with one pill became two. And then two twice a day. I wasn't actually fixing the problem or trying solutions — I was addressing the symptom. We do this all the time. With medicine, in parenting, with programs to address societal needs and frustrations. We see this with leadership teachings and philosophies too. Addressing symptoms is dangerous because we often feel like we accomplished something, we feel good, and the issue seems to go away. Add to it that with addressing symptoms, especially in leadership teaching and philosophies, they are REALLY close. It is never out of left field. The approach is often *one-degree off*. The problem with being *one-degree off* is later in the journey you find yourself miles off course. And, the problem you thought you solved comes back with a vengeance and often, like medicating the pain, with unintended and painful consequences. Don't settle for the idea that treating the symptoms or *one-degree off* approaches are good enough. Your life, the work you do, and the people you serve deserve solutions that truly work.

The following are some examples of *one-degree off* approaches I encountered on social media, and they are so NOT true, it makes me emotional just writing

A *distorted* view of reality leads to a *distorted* view of what's needed.

about it. I want to give two *one-degree off* approaches so we can learn from them. Hopefully, you can test and see what is good when you encounter seemingly good teachings that just *feel* off.

The first was a social media post with an insanely high response rate. The title of the post was "Selfless Leadership," so, naturally, I'm intrigued, right? And it was a beautifully written long post. But it was *one-degree off.* Which might as well have been 180 degrees off because the writer started to go through and describe selfless leadership and made it clear that leadership is not about the leader as an individual. So far, wonderful, beautiful, great... right?

Then paragraph by paragraph they continued to take the idea of selfless leadership being less about you to less of you. The writer argued that any of the individual characteristics, learned experiences, and authority that impacted others needed to be unlearned and removed. The writer continued to go through and systematically argue for and promote that true selfless leadership was the removal of one's self from the process.

She advocated for the removal of the leader. For 100% autonomous individuals and teams who could then co-labor or collaborate. Autonomy, self-directed teams, and collaboration are great things. These practices and leaders (or leadership) are not mutually exclusive. They are mutually beneficial. She positioned the leader as the problem. I understand we've all worked for very flawed, horrible bosses. It breaks my heart. It is why I do the work I do — I love leaders. I want them, their work, and their people to thrive. All of them. Not one at the detriment of the other.

We do need mission-driven leaders where it is about the work more than it is about them. We can all build a strong core of firm principles that benefit all involved, while softening our edges. We all benefit when we work together and have a say in our work. And at our best, we will still be Swiss cheese. Perfectly imperfect leaders and people with lots of holes. As you grow in Character, Relationships, and Skills (and begin to replace some myths) you will make it less *about* you — just don't bring less *of* you. Show up as you — who you are and how you are along with who you are becoming and how you are growing. The solution isn't removing all the leaders or bringing less of you — it is replacing the negative aspects of leadership and increasing the number of leaders who desire to serve the work and the people more than themselves.

The other painful *one-degree off* approach was a great graphic. It was so frustrating because it was a beautiful graphic. See for yourself:

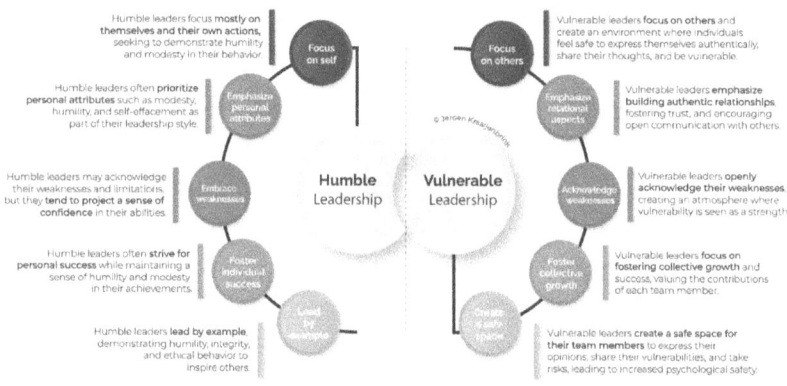

Humble vs. Vulnerable Leadership
The difference and why it matters

I marveled at the hundreds of people that reposted this. It was titled *Humble vs. Vulnerable Leadership* as the heading.[19] Well, I am a huge fan of both. I think we all benefit when we have both. I also thought, *"vs?"* How might they be at-odds with each other? The post proceeded to outline how humble leadership is detrimental. Detrimental because humble leaders focus on themselves and their own actions seeking to demonstrate modesty. Because they emphasize personal attributes (which furthers a focus on self), and that they embrace weaknesses but project a sense of confidence (again, them), and that they strive for personal success, and lead by example. Like Jacobim Mugatu in *Zoolander* I felt like I was taking crazy pills.[20] I couldn't connect how modesty, focusing on humility, and a confident approach to weaknesses was detrimental. I didn't understand their view of humility as an overemphasis on one's self.

Have you ever been around someone who had a false humility? What is false humility you ask? False humility would be when you promote and try to appear to have that particular virtue to a) trick people and ultimately manipulate them by gaining their trust and getting them to lower their guard, or b) humility done in a way that isn't true (e.g., a computer programmer who IS a great programmer dismissing their skills and abilities — "Oh, no, I'm no good. This, oh, it's nothing"). False humility a) is dangerous. Potentially some of the experience of the internet author that led them to portray humility this way. False humility b) is sometimes endearing, just not helpful or true. Humility and confidence. Humility and assertiveness. Humility and opinions. Humility and high standards. Humility and vulnerability can all coexist. And, in my humble experience, you do not get a vulnerable leader unless they are first humble. A summary of C.S. Lewis presents true humility as, "[...] *not thinking less of ourselves: it's thinking of ourselves less."* [21] When we think less about ourselves and how things may impact or benefit us (or the perception of us) we are free to lead, to serve, to be vulnerable, and to be humbly confident in our abilities and the work we do.

We also need vulnerable leadership. However, this graphic sets vulnerable leadership as the highest virtue. The misconceptions kept rolling from there. On the vulnerable side, they suggested that a vulnerable leader is totally focused on others. Interesting, because if you're being vulnerable, you're opening yourself up and you're usually paying more attention to what's going on with you. So, I see the message that the focus should be on others. Yet, the problem is the misuse of the word humility and the placing of vulnerability, not as A good thing but as THE best thing — it distorts our view of how they are connected and how each benefits us and others. In the end, I think the real truth is that good leaders have a right-sized view of themselves, and are strong enough to honestly express (and receive) true feelings, thoughts, and information when living in and fostering trust-based Relationships.

The problem with *one-degree off* approaches, and ideas like them, is that one degree is a small crack, but that small crack is like crack cocaine to the internet and people scrolling. Once that idea takes hold, the crack widens and infiltrates culture. The deeper it goes the more the middle disappears. We are left with two sides. A good side (your side, naturally). And, a bad side. And in the end we are left with one-sided over simplistic solutions to complex people problems and business problems. Resulting in unrealistic and untrue expectations or requirements of Servant Leaders that are so far from what's needed they are no longer helpful.

FALSE DICHOTOMIES FAIL, TENSION STRENGTHENS

Black and white thinking, oversimplification, is a sign that there is stress, fear, or hurt in the person or the system. And there is. Leaders are under tremendous pressure because of the public perceptions that they should get all the credit but also take all the blame. They are under pressure to perform, be perfect, and to be on display. The way we have set up leadership as command and control and as a position rather than an action creates stress and damage. So the oversimplification feels like a relief but really, it is a limitation. While holding a tension of opposites is more complex, it's a relief, too. It makes you stronger. As a Servant Leader, you don't have to pick humble or vulnerable, people or performance, boundaries or being kind. You can, and need to be both — for each of the pairs listed above and many more. When you do everyone and everything will be better for it.

Rarely, in life do we encounter true either/or scenarios. Either/or negates options and opportunities. Either/or divides and weakens. False either/or ideas about Servant Leaders are too simplistic. Too weak for something that requires such strength. We see it where humble versus vulnerable or selfless versus selfish are just too easy. They reduce leadership to a meme. Embrace the tension of AND instead of OR. Tension holds things together. When we approach with an AND not an OR, we unite, combine, and create. Tension makes things stronger. Tension honors the position leaders are in. The Herculean strength servant leadership truly requires.

Have you ever heard of the Hercules Hold? I hadn't. But, I've felt it.

How often do you feel like this as a leader?

The Hercules Hold is a *World's Strongest Man* event. In the Hercules Hold the athletes stand on a raised platform, grab onto two chains, and hold two pillars, each weighing 160 kg (~352 lbs). In the competition, kind of like it feels in leadership, there is no time limit. The event isn't over until the athlete can no longer hold both pillars.

I don't know about you, but when I look at that I get stressed, afraid of being ripped apart, and know trying to hold those pillars will hurt, or worse, would hurt someone if I dropped a pillar on them.

This image depicts the strength required to lead in the tension that is servant leadership. It also depicts the weight and responsibility leaders feel, and the forces that pull on leaders: People and performance. New business opportunities and our need for better training or more people. Advancing the mission and making sure we manage our money. Especially forces like what might be needed and what people tell me to do. What I feel is right and what culture tells me is right, wrong, and the way "it is supposed to be." What people say servant leadership is and what it truly is.

If we go back to my experience, to what I outlined in the first two sections of the book, we see the distorted view of servant leadership in our culture, and *that,* I definitely had. Honestly, I was a Misguided Servant. My personality (and Character, Relationships, and Skills deficits), what people told me servant leadership *had* to be, and the incomplete and inaccurate cultural narrative from the media made me think if I wasn't this Misguided Servant I would be seen as and become a Bad Boss.

I quickly discovered I wasn't alone here. That others were wrestling with people's perception and culture's narrative of who and how a Servant Leader should be. They were struggling with what type of leader they were if they weren't exactly the "Servant Leader" they were expected to be.

I also discovered the perceptions and narratives around servant leadership aren't real. They are myths, misconceptions and norms that lead us to be Misguided Servants, not Servant Leaders. These myths are also what likely keeps those we perceive as Bad Bosses from embracing servant leadership because of how distorted, "soft," and impossible to achieve it appears to them. And, for fear of being Bad Bosses, we go all in on the myths. Just like I realized when I heard feedback about my integrity, when we go all in as a Misguided Servant (just like if we went all in on being a Bad Boss) we actually diminish our integrity, influence, and impact as leaders.

Here are ten common myths about Servant Leaders that create Misguided Servants, what we avoid because it is how we perceive Bad Bosses, and true characteristics of Servant Leaders.

Misguided Servants	Servant Leaders	Bad Bosses
People-Pleasers	Mission-Driven	Self-Serving
Subservient	Needed Service	Grandiose
Utopian	Relentlessly Optimistic	Cynical
Nice	Kind Truth	Bossy
Always Available	Present	Unapproachable
Naive	Aware	Conniving
Permissive	Principled	Intolerant
Passive	Assertive	Aggressive
Avoid Power	Share Power Responsibly	Abuse Power
Bleeding Heart	Servant Heart. Business Mind.	It's Just Business

These false dichotomies, the either/or mentality of a Misguided Servant or Bad Boss, are honestly reinforced by the most endearing attributes of Servant Leaders — and our desire to be perceived as such. You know what I mean. Servant Leaders are nice. They don't Abuse Power. Sometimes we're People-Pleasers. We can be accused of having a Bleeding Heart. Because we desire to serve we are "always on," always available, and might struggle to say no. Since we're not above getting our hands dirty, taking out the trash, or sweeping the floor, we sometimes find ourselves stuck in the menial work and a potentially Subservient approach where instead of being humble we actually place our work (or ourselves) as less important than the people around us.

Here's how I added fuel to that fire in my life and leadership. Maybe you do, too. I desire to be and do those things (except for Subservient — but guilty of that too). They are good things. Instead of accepting them as GOOD things I made them THE things. The pillars of my identity, my integrity, my worth and brand as a leader. And I became Misguided. I also made the opposite Bossy things out to be the absolute worst things, wrong, and not very Servant Leader-like. Don't get me wrong here, that list is bad. I mean imagine someone who is absolutely Self-Serving, Cynical, Grandiose, Aggressive, and is the "It's Just Business" boss. That's terrible. Look closer though. Or from a different perspective. Like I did. Look for a one-degree switch to the positive. I realized too often I saw what is actually self-care as Self-Serving. Any negative comments as Cynical perspectives. And being strategic as being Conniving.

The same distortion that led me to be a Misguided Servant led me to see good, healthy leadership qualities like self-care, negative feedback, and strategy as Bad Boss qualities. To me, anything that was even in the vicinity of being "bossy" or appeared bad was written off as bad because of my fear of getting too close and going all in as a Bad Boss. What I couldn't see, and what makes so much difference is the motive, the complexity of the situation, countless factors from numerous angles, and how my own personality and experiences *might* be clouding my perception of what's really going on.

Truth be told, there was a lot more going on. There was too much weight on the pillars. I didn't yet have the Character, Relationships, and Skills to be able to lead in the tension. My limited experience plus the increasing weight of my leadership responsibility quickly revealed I couldn't hold the pillars. For fear of losing my grip altogether, even though I knew I was gripping on to being a Misguided Servant, I let go of the Bad Boss handle to avoid becoming the Bad Boss I so desperately tried not to be. So, even though it was painful, ineffective, and I knew it wasn't the best way — I took the Misguided approach, and believed the myth like it was reality.

Servant leaders are not *people pleasers.*

Servant leaders are *mission-driven.*

How do you think holding one 352 pound pillar went? You know how it went. I outlined it earlier in the book. It pulled me over, and destroyed my integrity. The very thing I prided myself on — honesty, was the thing that was being questioned (challenged). And rightfully so. I flew so far toward People-Pleasing that it actually became more important to me than honesty.

Imagine being that tired leader, standing on the raised platform, releasing the weight that feels so heavy, but is actually helping you balance, and grabbing the other pillar with both hands. It doesn't matter who you are, you are getting pulled off that platform and it is going to hurt.

The hurt finally led me to investigate what was really going on. The hurt, the pain even, of having my integrity questioned led me to discover my conflict avoidance came from a combination of personality, upbringing, and pride. I discovered my rose-colored glass optimism actually influences people to be more realistic, more negative even, to balance me out and try to tether to reality. Examples of other leaders I deeply admired showed me a stronger, more mission-driven, relentlessly hopeful way to lead and to serve. Through practice, goal setting, and getting people around me to support me, plus some (lots of) crises, setbacks, challenges, studying of leadership, promotions, and successes I began replacing some of the oversimplified stereotypes of servant leadership and found the strength to lead in the tension. This created the opportunity to see what it's like to serve a great purpose, serve people, create profits, and adhere to the principles that guide me.

Here's the best part. Through your strengthened Character, Relationships, and Skills plus the myths, misconceptions, and norms we are about to dismantle you can and will have the strength *and* the knowledge about the true characteristics of Servant Leadership you need to stand on that platform and hold (lead in and with) the proper tension between serving and leading.

Let's replace the myths that do not serve well and dive into the aspects of servant leadership that will enable you to lead with integrity, grow your influence, and deliver impactful results. Here's the great news that I didn't realize when I first began this work. As a Servant Leader, you are already fantastic, Skilled, and agile enough to be able to hold what appear to be two contradictory things together, serve and lead. I know, it makes sense to you, but for many they are contradictory, not complementary ideals. That ability, combined with us spending the first part of this book redefining servant leadership and walking through the need and combination of Character,

Relationships, and Skills, means you are ready to replace the myths that do not serve.

For each myth you will see the myth, what we're told that creates Misguided Servants, the Bad Boss qualities we aim to avoid, and what to replace it with for true servant leadership. You will see examples of what it looks like in real-life scenarios and each myth will conclude with what attributes — Character, Relationships, and Skills — are needed and how you can focus on growing in those areas to successfully hold the tension in a creative and productive way to grow as a Servant Leader. Let's dive into myth #1: Servant Leaders are People-Pleasers.

To see the table for Misguided Servants, Bad Bosses, and Servant Leaders as you go through each myth, visit www.redefineyourservantleadership.com.

MYTH #1
SERVANT LEADERS ARE PEOPLE-PLEASERS

A Misguided Servant is a People-Pleaser.
A Bad Boss is Self-Serving.
Replace both with: *Servant Leaders are Mission-Driven.*

Mission Driven

People-Pleasers   Self-Serving

If all you do is go around trying to keep people happy, you will fail. No amount of Skill will ever make (or keep) everybody happy. Trying to please people will not move projects forward, or give people the job and pay they want. Even if you find success for a second, you won't be happy. And worse, because different things please different people and sometimes what pleases one, conflicts with what pleases another, you will quickly find yourself down the slippery slope of compromising your integrity — to yourself, your principles, and your work. No, Servant Leaders are not People-Pleasers. Servant leaders are Mission-Driven.

Mission-Driven Servant Leaders take a *mission first, people always* approach. This approach enables you to serve a greater purpose than yourself, for the benefit of the people involved. When the mission comes first you can humble yourself to a purpose, an objective, and values that are larger (and more enduring) than you — or any one person. Through your Mission-Driven POV (purpose, objective, and values) you see how to serve people in and through the work. You gain the perspective you need (and permission) to say no. To say no in service of something greater. To stop pleasing unpleasable people. And, to say no to someone because that no is for their benefit.

The tension of the Mission-Driven, that is *mission first, people always,* approach influences your prioritization of people over other aspects of the work, the decisions you make, and how you go about doing the work and treating people because, ultimately, your goal isn't to please — it is to influence people toward a shared purpose that brings a benefit. Benefits like lives saved in an operating room, student success and achievement, a training to improve collaboration and communication in the office, or personal and professional success and growth that impacts one's well-being.

When you're Mission-Driven, you can serve the overall goal and the long-term vision, not merely aim to please people or produce pleasing results in the short term. This perspective allows you and the people you lead to sacrifice. To put off instant gratification for larger, more meaningful results that truly make a difference.

And because it is about the mission, not merely being the one who pleases or serves people, you can actually be served as well. You can (and need) to receive from others. It is better to give than receive, yes! But, how selfish might it be if you don't allow others to serve you? People who can and want to help you miss out on the opportunity, and you miss out on what they have to offer, when service is only a one-way street.

What are some aspects of the Character, Relationships, Skills attributes important for being Mission-Driven?**

Character

→   Establish a strong, healthy connection to larger missions, guiding principles, and beliefs.

Relationships

→   Foster a team approach to driving the mission forward, while providing trusting autonomy and loving accountability for all.

Skills

→   Communicate a clear, compelling vision for the desired future and the impact possible through a collaborative, Mission-Driven approach.

**These, and the following for each of the myths, are by no means an exhaustive list. You will find key example growth areas at the end of each myth. Use them to as you replace the myth, allow them to influence your growth and leadership.

MYTH #2
SERVANT LEADERS MUST BE SUBSERVIENT

A Misguided Servant is Subservient.
A Bad Boss is Grandiose.
Replace both with: *Servant Leaders do the Needed Service.*

Needed Service

Subservient   Grandiose

I get it. In an expression of humility and the opportunity to lead by example we want to show we are not too good for something or someone, and we want to show the type of work ethic we have and desire to see in others. I commend you. We lose our way when we lose why we do it, when we get stuck doing it, or when we subordinate the value of seemingly menial work (or ourselves) under other work (or people). The problem with losing our way and our why when we visibly get our hands dirty, get stuck doing it, or place other work (or people) in a higher position is that we reinforce those who do grandstand and we miss out on what's actually needed and how we can help.

As a Servant Leader, you provide Needed Service. Seek out the highly Needed Service, whether it is taking out trash or talking strategy in a board meeting. You need to get into the messy work — it displays your Character and increases your influence. Doing what needs to be done — what is needed in the moment to move the mission forward demonstrates support and care. You simply don't stop at hopping from need to need. You seek out how to best serve as a leader. The best service you can provide may be taking out the trash and it may be planning the strategy. All the work performed toward a just cause is meaningful and necessary — as a leader you must determine what is your highest level contribution to what's needed at that time, and help others find and operate in theirs as well.

When you focus on Needed Service the perception of what *might* be happening and the cultural pressure of titles, hierarchies, and positions fade away. You realize the camaraderie, benefit, and joy that comes when a bunch of people who don't care about "being somebody," who love helping everybody, will serve anybody. This is the type of Needed Service that will change the lives of your customers, team members, neighbors, and families.

From the breakroom to the boardroom, packing boxes to planning strategy, answering calls or calling people to act — *always serve, and serve all ways.*

What are some aspects of the Character, Relationships, Skills attributes important for doing the Needed Service?

Character

→ Look beyond one's own self to what's needed, and to confidently say "yes" and "no" to serve priority needs.

Relationships

→ Build mutually-beneficial Relationships sharing responsibility by giving and receiving so each person makes their highest contribution.

Skills

→ Owning and investing in your unique expertise, gifts, and talents and using them to serve the highest need.

MYTH #3
SERVANT LEADERS ARE UTOPIAN

A Misguided Servant is Utopian.
A Bad Boss is Cynical.
<u>Replace</u> both with: *Servant Leaders are Relentlessly Optimistic.*

Relentlessly Optimistic

Utopian   Cynical

Mission-Driven, Servant Leaders can be misconstrued as Utopian, pie in the sky, and the rose colored glasses type because of the ever-present hope for a bright, better future. We may also be guilty of avoiding negative feedback. You know, when someone changes any negative word like "weaknesses" to "opportunities" for fear of deflating people. Or won't *ever* paint things as bad for fear of turning people off to them or their work. Sometimes, we don't even think we can have doubts about if things might actually work. For fear of being Cynical we take the role of tireless cheerleader and our one-sided point of view leads others to doubt us and our work anyway. Neither are helpful. Neither are realistic.

I had a client, Diane, who has since passed away. Years ago, a consultant visited and told her everything she needed to do at the school (she was the director) in order to make it all perfect. She was an eternal optimist, and I think her feet only touched the ground about three times in her 78 year life. And, you might be thinking her response would be equally Utopian, but it was not. She told the consultant, "That's nice, but I have to deal with the reality that is." She was neither Utopian, nor was she willing to be Cynical. What she was was Relentlessly Optimistic. Things can be bad, there can be real fears, but a Relentlessly Optimistic leader sees where they are broken, works to fix them, and chooses hope all throughout.

Choosing hope in the face of pain, adversity, and potentially life-threatening realities isn't just nice — it turns out it's necessary. Have you ever heard of the Stockdale Paradox? In his book, *Good to Great,* Jim Collins introduces us to Admiral Jim Stockdale. He was the highest-ranking United States military officer in the "Hanoi Hilton" prisoner-of-war camp during the Vietnam War. He was tortured over twenty times during his eight-year imprisonment. He had no idea if he would be released, or when. But, he kept in his mind the Relentlessly Optimistic belief that he would not only get out, but would turn this imprisonment into something that mattered in his life and the world. When asked what the personality traits were of the people who did not make it out of the camp alive, he was very clear that false optimism kills. He said that the people who did not make it were the ones who would convince themselves "We'll be out by Christmas." And when that date came and went too many times they would lose hope, and die of a broken heart.[22]

Real leaders deal with what is really in front of them. Then, they choose to lead positively — in their approach, style, and disposition — because of the hope they have in and for the future. When you have hope and faith that you will succeed, plus the willingness to face the facts about what's really going on, have the courage to establish and enforce boundaries, you will create better plans, solve problems faster, and encourage others — through your example of courage — that success isn't just a hope — it is in fact possible. The work you do — changing the world in a positive way — dismantling human trafficking rings, bringing clean drinking water to over 8 BILLION people, or sharing the Gospel to all people in all nations come with significant adversities and challenges. To avoid the physical, emotional, spiritual, financial, or infrastructure realities would be a disservice to the work and the people. The bigger and brighter the beautiful future you see as possible, the more *Relentlessly* Optimistic the person needs to be to lead the way. In the face of fear, choose hope. Be Relentlessly Optimistic.

What are some aspects of the Character, Relationships, Skills attributes important for being Relentlessly Optimistic?

Character

→ Embrace reality as it is, and orient yourself toward the good, the positive, and what is desired.

Relationships

→ Identify growth-oriented Relationships and cultivate the ability to speak truth, challenge, encourage, and call to act.

Skills

→ Develop the ability to accept things and people as they are, and work toward what is possible.

MYTH #4
SERVANT LEADERS MUST BE NICE

A Misguided Servant must be Nice.
A Bad Boss is Bossy.

<u>Replace</u> both with: *Servant Leaders tell the Kind Truth.*

Kind Truth

|————————————————————————————————|

Nice   Bossy

So, this is likely the single biggest myth influencing servant leadership today. Why didn't I make it Myth #1? Because it was important for us to replace the idea that Servant Leaders are Utopian, Subservient, People-Pleasers. Now you probably see how impossible always being Nice will be while leading Mission-Driven, Needed Service, with a Relentlessly Optimistic outlook. The good news is it's a myth that if you are not Nice, you are automatically Bossy. In fact, being Nice was never mentioned in *The Servant as Leader* by Robert Greenleaf, even though we may be led to believe *Nice* is the hidden 11th characteristic of Servant Leaders — thou shalt be Nice. Why is this idea so pervasive? Because Servant Leaders are ridiculously kind — they display empathy, listen well, serve, and focus on community. These are real Skills that aren't found in all people and places. However, Servant Leaders are also truthful, direct, focused, have strategy, and hold themselves and others to a high standard. So that might be construed as Bossy by some. It is not an either or, because Servant Leaders are not tied to a perception or politeness — they are about the mission, the people and the truth, and sharing it in a way that serves those who hear it.

I have to admit I am a recovering People-Pleaser, and I like being Nice. Niceness is much better than impoliteness. We should be Nice as often as possible. The problem, I realized, was sometimes my being Nice got in the way of being honest. It is much easier to be Nice than to tell the Kind Truth. Why? Because sometimes the Kind Truth is hard. I realized when push came to shove me being Nice was more about what you thought of me, not how I was helping you. That's right, being Nice is often because I care more about what you think of me, where being kind shows how much I think of and care about you.

I would withhold helpful, kind feedback for fear of being thought to be a jerk. I would struggle to work up the courage to tell someone what they were doing was wrong for fear of losing the relationship. My niceness began to impact my integrity, you saw this in the opening of this book, and again in the previous chapter. That is when I realized that to better serve people I must choose the truth. Still, I feared becoming a Bossy truth-teller. Truthing people up and down the halls. You know the type, the "No disrespect, but…" followed by absolute disrespect that may or may not be true — but definitely opinionated. I watched and studied and saw leaders combine their love of people and truth and deliver it kindly. I realized that Servant Leaders can be Nice, and that Servant Leaders do tell the Kind Truth.

Because Servant Leaders do focus on people, because they have the Skills to communicate, what they actually do is tell the Kind Truth. The Kind Truth, as difficult as it may be to say to somebody as you're sitting across from them, will benefit them. The truth may be hard to hear, but it is never devoid of value. Telling them that Kind Truth instead of withholding it so that you can be Nice, artificially keep harmony, and so they will like you is not serving anyone except for yourself. Right? In the face of being Nice or being direct, you might slide left or right but in the middle is the most impactful way to be. Courageously demonstrate your integrity and care for the mission and the people by sharing the Kind Truth.

What are some aspects of the Character, Relationships, Skills attributes important for telling the Kind Truth?

Character

→ Prioritize being a person who shares the full truth and values respect over hearing good things and keeping people happy.

Relationships

→ Create trust-based Relationships where giving and receiving feedback is valued and requested.

Skills

→ Practice communicating the complete, hard truth clearly and with care.

MYTH #5
SERVANT LEADERS MUST BE ALWAYS AVAILABLE

A Misguided Servant is Always Available.
A Bad Boss is Unapproachable.

<u>Replace</u> both with: *Servant Leaders are Present.*

Present

Always Available	Unapproachable

Let's go into another myth we need to replace — and quickly. It is spinning out of control. Not just for Servant Leaders — for all of us. It is the myth that we must be Always Available. The pressure to be Always Available has grown exponentially with the rise of sayings like "I have an open door policy" with the shift to open offices, and potentially the most invasive — technology. Our tech has the power to make us available 24/7, tell people if and when we are Available, and the lure of it has taken away our power to power it down. The leaping to conclusions of what is going on if someone might not be Available are outrageous. If not Available it is assumed one is Unapproachable, not working as hard, or doesn't *really* care. This boundaryless epidemic is frying all of us out and leaving shells of us always around and never really there. The Always Available culture doesn't serve anyone. It's time to prioritize being Present, instead of always being available.

You might be thinking, but what if I miss an opportunity to help someone, to get a donation, to make that deal, to make a difference? You're right, you might miss it. What about if I need something and my team member isn't available or they don't respond when I need them too? That does happen. My question is, what opportunities might be available that we are missing because we are not Present?

Being Always Available, always on, puts all of us at a heightened level of stress. The guilt of not working or fear of missing out (FOMO) actually makes us inaccessible for the most important people in our lives, not to mention the most important work. It is ruining organizations too. Organizations are losing great people because of the need to be Always Available. We've felt this most through the rise of work-life balance conversations and the great resignation. People are Always Available to the point of burnout when they break down and leave or break down entirely.

I believe it comes first from a place deep, deep down where we want to help. We want to serve. We really do not like to see people struggle, be left out, or see jobs left undone. We desire things to be perfect. Being Always Available will not make them perfect, but being Present might be the perfect way to engage in each moment.

Think back to times with people. To when you got lost in the work. When you said no to something or someone because of something more important. It is freeing. Rewarding even. You probably have the deepest connection with those people. And delivered your best work then. You didn't experience FOMO you experienced freedom to engage and enjoy. It is up to you to replace the myth and make this change for yourself. Establish time when you work and when you don't. Then work HARD when you do, and don't when you don't. When focusing on the priorities in your life — truly focus on them. Build the rhythm you need to rest to lead at your best. Then, give it your all when you're on and give yourself permission to be off when you're off.

As a leader, lead others to prioritize being Present and Available. Let them know you're making a change. Invite them to change too. Use your influence to drive change at work. It may be slow, most things that are worth it take time. Be the one who hits deadlines, but who doesn't email 9–5 employees at 11pm. The one who tunes out on vacation and trusts people to take care of it all. Begin deviceless meetings and discuss important decisions and commit to meaningful action. Close your laptop and turn away from the desk toward the person when they come in to meet with you. Create the connection needed to form trusting Relationships and improve employee engagement and retention. Serve where you are. Lead where you are. Create a culture where the people you work with can too.

Being Present requires you are not elsewhere. Not physically, of course, you can't be in two places at once. But, also in your heart and your mind. If your heart desires to be elsewhere your mind will go there. It requires an intentional act of service, devotion even, to the work or the person in front of you. Using all of your Skills to focus, listen, communicate, discern, to engage and respond to what is going on and what may be needed. Being Present doesn't mean you're Unapproachable, it means you approach what you do with purpose and on purpose. When you are Present you get to truly see how to best lead and how to use your Character, Relationships, and Skills to make an impact through work and in the life of the person you're with. It takes practice, it is hard, and where you are intentionally Present you will act with the most integrity, gain the most influence, and be able to make the greatest difference.

What are some aspects of the Character, Relationships, Skills attributes important for being Present?

Character

→   Outline boundaries that are firm, not rigid, so you can separate yourself, focus on your needs, priorities, and the needs of others.

Relationships

→   Seek out connection and camaraderie, request what you need and honor the needs of others.

Skills

→   Focus on actively listening and asking clarifying questions during conversations.

MYTH #6
SERVANT LEADERS ARE NAIVE

A Misguided Servant is Naive.
A Bad Boss is Conniving.
Replace both with: *Servant Leaders are Aware.*

Aware

|———|
Naive   Conniving

There's this misconception out there that Servant Leaders are, or almost have to be, Naive to undertake such a thing as servant leadership. A kind of "hear no evil, see no evil, do no evil" mentality. And, in the business world especially, they appear oblivious to how *it* really works. Maybe you've felt it. A bit of the pat on the head and "bless your heart" you don't know how the world actually works. Problem is too often we help make that case. I know I have. By avoiding looking at the finances, saying things like "Don't tell me, I don't want to know," or choosing the head in the sand approach hoping it blows by. It isn't helpful to be Naive, and if you're not Naive it doesn't mean you are or will be Conniving, coercive, power or money hungry. Choosing to be Naive is a choice to not use all that you have. Choose to be Aware.

Imagine if another person or organization was trying to organize a hostile takeover of your business. Wouldn't you want to know? It doesn't mean you must fight fire with fire, but it does give you what you need to respond. If you were going to run out of money and fail to make payroll wouldn't you want to know? Knowing your numbers deeply and working to produce profits to sustain the business and support the people makes you responsible, not money hungry. If there was a critical threat to the business or an opportunity to honestly acquire another business wouldn't you want to know? The information required to avoid issues or act on opportunities doesn't make you sly, it allows you to be thinking strategically. When you are Aware you make better choices, and you can always choose how you respond.

Your choice and response may just influence others to positively change how they choose to respond to trying situations.

Without awareness how do you know if you are operating with integrity? Because the responsibility of leading is so great and your service to the mission and people is so important you should always be ready to give an answer to whomever asks. When you are ready with the honest answer you can operate in your integrity, yes. But the very act of sharing then serves as an example and empowers others to know and act in the same way moving forward. Awareness gives you the power to navigate through your principles, chart the best strategic option, and show others the way.

Your presence produces awareness. That's right. Because you are Present you no longer are able to play the Naive card. You cannot help but be Aware if you are Present. In Myth #5 we replaced Always Available with being Present. When you are Present in the work, with people, and with yourself you will gain the awareness you need to lead. When Present you pull the thread. *(Remember this from the Communication Skill?)* You reflect on how you are feeling, what you're thinking, or what action might be needed. With others you ask the second question. "'How are you?' *'Good'* " Leads to a response from you like, "Great. What makes today so good?".

The second question gives you the insight, perspective, connection you need to lead and serve. And, to get answers about people, problems, and possibilities you'd never know otherwise. When you are Present you pay attention. When you pay attention you ask questions. When you ask questions you gain awareness. You discover new things. Just because you have all the information and "inside scoop" doesn't mean you are Conniving, but without the information you can never be strategic. Without awareness you won't see what doesn't add up and gain the opportunity to learn about it, to avoid problems, or correct what's going wrong.

While naivety allows you to get by and get the benefit of the doubt, your honesty, compassion, choices, when you are in fact Aware, removes all doubt about your Character and dedication to how you lead. Choose to be Aware.

What are some aspects of the Character, Relationships, Skills attributes important for being Aware?

Character

→ Model and expect transparent communication, where each party assumes positive intent until proven otherwise.

Relationships

→ Model and expect transparent communication, where each party assumes positive intent until proven otherwise.

Skills

→ Welcome information and seek to continuously gain knowledge — content and context — so you can discern the best and most appropriate course of action.

MYTH #7
SERVANT LEADERS ARE PERMISSIVE

A Misguided Servant is Permissive.
A Bad Boss is Intolerant.

Replace both with: *Servant Leaders are Principled.*

Principled

Permissive	Intolerant

The pressure to permit everything is overwhelming. You're told if you're not Permissive, you're Intolerant. You can choose to not accept something or someone's action without being Intolerant of the individual. Really, when you do, you show how much that person truly means to you. Being Intolerant or completely Permissive does not serve anyone. If everything goes, then we will never know what actually goes, what's important, and how we can best understand and engage with each other. And if it is all rigid, inflexible policies applied without thought to the situation or the person we lose out on the opportunity to build a connected, committed community of people striving to achieve a shared purpose. Replace a Permissive (or Intolerant) approach with a Principled approach. A Principled approach gives everyone involved — you, others, the organization — the ability to operate with integrity, build stronger connections to the ideal and to the individuals.

Our principles are the guiding truth, values, and behaviors of each of us, and of our workplaces. They serve as the foundation for who we are and how we act as people and organizations. They give us the operating framework to reproduce the type of Character and actions we desire, individually and organizationally. Principles influence our culture, guide decisions, and drive others' interest, or disinterest, in us and our workplace. We need guiding principles — as people and organizations — to give ourselves and our people a map to why, how, and what we do.

Many of the concepts in this book are principles. *Mission first, people always. Servant Heart. Business Mind (it's coming — Myth #10). Be Relentlessly*

Optimistic. Other examples include things like: *Second mile service, Disrupt yourself first, Always be growing, Choose kindness, Be slow to speak and quick to listen, Spend less than you make,* or *Treat others like you wish to be treated.* We need to lead with principles to truly serve the mission, the people, and keep what's possible possible.

Ryan, a new CEO, and coaching client of mine, was facing a challenging personnel situation. Julie was a beloved, tenured team member who repeatedly failed to meet the goals and expectations. Ryan asked what she needed, offered support, clarified expectations, and gave her time to improve. Sadly, Julie was not working well with the people she led, and she was not delivering the results needed. Ryan realized the longer he did nothing the more this situation was negatively impacting the team's morale and performance. He was worried that soon it would impact their ability to run safe, caring programs for children. He felt like he was between a rock and a hard place wanting to maintain the organization's high standard for safety and operational excellence and treating other people like he'd want to be treated. He knew what he needed to do, but it was Thanksgiving.

Here's what he said on our call, "Have you ever experienced someone being let go right before Christmas?"

Me: "No."

Ryan: "Well, I have. It sucks. You just don't do that to people. You know. It isn't right."

Me: "That's tough. So, given that, what do you want to do in this situation?"

Ryan: "Well, I am not going to let her go before Christmas. That's for sure!"

Me: "Okay, great. I commend you for sticking with your principles. I'm curious, what's the impact of this decision?"

The cost to Ryan and his organization was about 40% of her annual salary.

Would you want to pay someone for five months of work if they worked for six weeks?

Because of certain company salary and severance policies the decision to *not* fire her before Christmas cost Ryan and his organization five months of her salary, instead of a couple weeks' worth of money. BUT, what they gained was worth much more than that.

Ryan was able to demonstrate to his team, especially his senior leaders, how important safety, excellence, and treating people with compassion — prioritizing them above the bottom line — was to him and the organization. In a time period where many organizations in their industry struggled with revenue and retention — they thrived. By leaning into and maintaining this Principled approach, they've retained (and reclaimed) team members, they are serving more children today, plus they've grown their gross revenue 25% (which equals multiple millions of dollars) in just under 2 years (industry average is about 3–5% growth annually). Still, the greatest impact may be seen in the response one senior leader had much later to a family health crisis of another team member. The company policy said no paid time off. Their guiding principles said otherwise. Before Ryan could intervene, that senior leader, and others, figured out a way to get her time off, build a plan for paid FMLA, and create a "sick bank" where team members could contribute paid sick days to support each other. When Ryan asked them about it they responded, "We want to treat other people like we'd want to be treated, right?"

Principles are the path to operating with personal and professional integrity in complex, confusing situations where there is no one right or wrong way. While there may not be one right or wrong way for you and your organization there is still a best way. The way that honors the work you do, how you do it, and the people you do it with. Your principles may not be for others. That's okay. They are your principles. Your organization's principles may not be for everyone. That's okay. They are your organization's principles. The best principles are not for everyone, but can benefit everyone. Principles allow us to serve each situation, individually, with care for what's going on and the people involved. Principles give people the opportunity to adopt, to connect, and to grow through shared beliefs and behaviors that in turn permit people to work even more autonomously and effectively to achieve great things.

What are some aspects of the Character, Relationships, Skills attributes important for being Principled?

Character

→ Develop and consistently model the principles, values, and behaviors that are acceptable and consistent with your Character.

Relationships

→ Create supportive Relationships with people who align with your principles while embracing the differences others' offer.

Skills

→ Communicate clearly and often the principles that are considered acceptable within the organization, holding accountable where necessary.

MYTH #8
SERVANT LEADERS ARE PASSIVE

A Misguided Servant is Passive.
A Bad Boss is Aggressive.
<u>Replace</u> both with: *Servant Leaders are Assertive.*

Assertive

Passive   Aggressive

The myth that Servant Leaders are Passive is quite comical. As we've already said, leadership is an action. Leadership by nature isn't Passive. But we're not talking about action or inaction like that. No, we're talking about accepting or allowing what happens or what others do without response or even resistance. There are, no doubt, times where remaining Passive is the best option, especially when it doesn't involve you or the impact is inconsequential. The problem with Passive being the preferred (or only) approach is passivity for too long leads to pain, resentment, and aggression. The need to address the issue will come out, even if indirectly.

We all know the term passive-aggressive. Saying one thing and meaning another. The sudden explosion from Passive to Aggressive moves the harm being done from you to the object (or person). Passive aggressive behavior puts us in the Drama Triangle — where someone is a victim, someone is a villain, and someone is a savior. It doesn't serve anyone and there is no good way out. It harms them, hurts your integrity, and damages relationships in the process. Be Assertive to avoid becoming Aggressive.

A Passive approach at work, in business, doesn't work. We never make the sale. We wait for others to tell us what to do (and then complain that they do). Eventually, our businesses get disrupted by Assertive, innovative leaders in the industry and we fail to achieve the mission and serve people because of being Passive. This is why Servant Leaders need to be Assertive.

Let's just look at some of the attributes, approaches, and examples of what a Servant Leader may be asserting. They may assert the importance of prioritizing people over profits, products, or processes. They may assert that Character is more important than Skill. They assert themselves when a decision is final. Servant leaders take responsibility for their own mistakes and assert that others need to as well. They assert that treating others with dignity and respect is non-negotiable. That honesty is the best policy. That it is right for everyone to have clean drinking water. That you need to honor someone's boundary. That murder is wrong. That stealing isn't tolerated. *That everyone is created equal.*

In a circumstance where aggression was justified, assertiveness for one's self, what is right, and the needs of others changed the world.

It was a cold night, December 3, 1955, and a woman got on a bus. She sat down. She, and three other men sat in the same row. She was Black, as were the three men sitting in the same row as her. They were sitting in the first row of the "Colored section" of the bus. As others got on the bus the bus driver, James Blake, came back and told everybody in that row they needed to move back so he could create a larger "White section" on the bus.

This was not the first time this woman had been asked to move to the back by this bus driver. Years earlier, after paying her fare, this woman was asked to exit the bus and enter through the rear entrance. She did not. She chose to go home another way. And this time, she chose another way to assert what is right.

Now, whether what the bus driver demanded was lawful or not, does not matter, it was and is wrong. When he asked the four Black people in the first row of the "Colored section" to move, three of them got up and moved. One of them chose not to get up.

Her name was Rosa Parks. With a gentle strength, no disrespect, no aggression, and no bending to the ludicrous, demoralizing order she asserted what was good, right, and needed. This purposefully assertive act landed her in jail, yes. It also started the Montgomery Bus Boycott, thought of as the first large-scale protest against segregation in America. Her assertiveness also led to the calling of a young preacher to lead the charge. His name. Martin Luther King, Jr. who is often regarded as one of the great Servant Leaders in all of history. We are indebted to Rosa Parks' assertiveness in the face of injustice.[23]

When we are Passive about what is wrong and what will improve life for others, we miss the opportunity to serve and make a difference in the world. Assertiveness doesn't need to be forceful, and it might not be as effective if it is. It can be gentle while strong in conviction. You can speak assertively about your beliefs, values, and opinions without beating others up. When you demonstrate courage and conviction with a compassionate approach you gain respect, influence, and your words and actions have even greater impact.

What are some aspects of the Character, Relationships, Skills attributes important for being Assertive?

Character

→   Act courageously, respectfully, and wisely in accordance with your convictions about what's needed.

Relationships

→   Cultivate respect through compassion and honoring the values, beliefs and opinions of others.

Skills

→   Learn to speak with clear, confident authority, without aggression or disrespect, especially for personal needs, needs of others, and matters of importance.

MYTH #9
SERVANT LEADERS MUST AVOID POWER

A Misguided Servant Avoids Power.
A Bad Boss Abuses Power.

Replace both with: *Servant Leaders Share Power Responsibly.*

Share Power Responsibly

Avoid Power   Abusing Power

Power is unavoidable. Each of us has power. The myth that Servant leaders must Avoid Power is false, and impossible. Yes, of course, avoiding the abuse of power is a tenant of leading as a servant, but not avoiding it altogether. The thing is our power grows as we do. As you grow in Character, Relationships, and Skills you will naturally have more power over yourself and thus the situations you are in. As leaders, the more responsibility we take on the more power is attributed (or given) to us. On the flip side of that, with great power comes great responsibility (Thanks, Uncle Ben). The responsibility to not abuse, but also to not avoid. Instead, to avoid both extremes, Servant Leaders Share Power Responsibly.

As Servant Leaders we are responsible to the mission and responsible to the people. This means we must be responsible with the power given to us. Abdicating that authority would be irresponsible, just like a tyrannical approach, even in the name of a good cause, is irresponsible and harmful. Think about other places in life where you are responsible for important things — a friend's wedding, watching someone's child, borrowing a very expensive car or piece of jewelry. You don't NOT show up, let them wander aimlessly, or share it with other people all willy-nilly. You accept the responsibility, you try to show honor and care, and you share it with other people if and when there is a high level of trust. The same is true here. The power you have as a leader is entrusted to you — because of your Character, Relationships, and

Skills — and it is up to you to accept it, to honor and care for the gift given to you, and to share it responsibly.

It strikes me that another tenant of servant leadership is to empower others. However, if we avoid power we cannot actually empower. Because to empower is to give, to push power to others. On the podcast, *At The Table with Patrick Lencioni,* in the *Stop Using the E Word* episode he talked about another leadership book and the idea of empowerment. He cited the book as saying that a leader gives away power. When we are empowering we are pushing power out to others. This is the type of sharing power that is required of Servant Leaders. You give of something you have to benefit the mission and the people. To do this, you must first accept the power, authority even, that you have because of your leadership, position, or influence.

When you choose to responsibly use the power you have, honoring and caring for the work and the people, then you can truly share it. Because of the power for good and for harm that power produces, you know the thing that serves best is to be responsible with whom you share it. It would be irresponsible to give the power to negatively impact someone else's livelihood to an irresponsible person. In our companies, that's what we're talking about. When we place managers (or leaders) over divisions, decisions, or people we are giving them power that will positively or negatively impact the life of another human. Look for people of integrity, with impeccable character, with a track record of great work and decisions. Look for someone that people already follow, even without the power and position. Then, give them the power (authority) to lead, to make decisions, to act in alignment with mission, values, for the people. Now, together, you can share the load and hold the tension — being accountable to one another, to the work, and the people you serve.

As you Share Power Responsibility, your influence grows. You are attributed even more power, or authority, which empowers you to lead even further outside of your direct sphere of influence, and create an unavoidable, powerful, and positively impactful ripple effect.

What are some aspects of the Character, Relationships, Skills attributes important for Sharing Power Responsibly?

Character

➜ Accept the authority and responsibility of leadership, while honoring that of others. Humbly use power to serve the mission and the people.

Relationships

➜ Build Relationships where communication and feedback fuel trust, practice asking for what you need from people.

Skills

➜ Delegate responsibility, authority, and share power so others may lead, decide, and act.

MYTH #10
SERVANT LEADERS HAVE A BLEEDING HEART

A Misguided Servant has a Bleeding Heart.
A Bad Boss says, "It's Just Business."

<u>Replace</u> both with: *Servant Leaders use their Servant Heart and Business Mind.*

Servant Heart. Business Mind.

|←——→|
Bleeding Heart   It's Just Business

This one just runs rampant in the culture, especially in the serving professions and industries. There is this idea that to be a Servant Leader you must have a Bleeding Heart to the exclusion of any kind of business skills or goals. There's a belief that there should be no business strategy, metrics, bottom line or any other concern because then you are just all about the business and don't care about people. There is a disgust, an intolerance even, to a "No" decision when it means not doing a program, helping a person, or funding a project even if the realities of the organization — strategy, resources, capacity don't support it. We can only act based on our compassion and care for people. If you were to say "no, we don't have the money, no, we don't have the time, no, we don't have the resources," then it is all of a sudden, Just Business. You're just like everybody else. You've been playing this false game, saying you're a Servant Leader and that you care, but you don't.

Have you ever heard of a ventricular rupture? It is in fact, a Bleeding Heart. Do you know the most common outcome? Death. That's right. An unrestrained Bleeding Heart means eventually, you die. Unrestrained benevolence and all generosity is unsustainable. On the flip side, the "It's Just Business" approach of the corporate culture since 1980 does not work. It leaves us all with a broken heart. Go grab any statistic on employee loyalty, retention, engagement, even productivity. If it is all about money, it becomes all about the individual (yes, each of us out for ourselves) and people lose sight of mission, the passion fades, and eventually it becomes a lifeless j-o-b.

We started these myths with: Servant Leaders are Mission-Driven. This approach enables you to serve a greater purpose than yourself, for the benefit of the people involved. When the mission comes first you can humble yourself to serve with a Servant Heart relentlessly striving for what's possible. Through your Business Mind you grow the mission, the bottom line, and the amount of service, generosity, and charity you can provide to people. Far more and far longer than a Bleeding Heart can provide. A Servant Heart, Business Mind approach is the sustainable, continuously reinforcing process to lasting impact.

Servant Leaders have the advantage here when they approach their work with a Servant Heart and a Business Mind. Yes, the work we do is for people. And, we do want to empower and focus on the well-being and growth of our people. Yes, we want them to flourish. And, we do believe that treating our people well leads to great results and that developing our people does, in fact, develop our business. We do hold that going out and being generous in the service that we do, regardless of resources, is a good thing. And it doesn't mean that unequivocally unabashedly, we always get to do whatever we want. It means there is still restraint and that there are still boundaries, and that there still is discernment that is required inside of these things to properly and effectively choose what to do.

Sometimes, to be effective we have to say "that's not our problem to solve." Or "we would like to do this, however, we don't have the resources to be able to address that at this time." If those things are true, that's okay. It is really okay. We are not just organically serving — we are in fact serving a specific mission and we cannot take care of everything that breaks our hearts and be effective in the end. To have the biggest impact, we don't lead with just a Bleeding Heart or just a business mind — but with a Servant Heart and Business Mind.

Where does true integrity, influence, and impact lie? It's when you take a Servant's Heart and a Business Mind and combine them in a leader who desires to do things for others, for the mission, for the people, and for themselves. They have a heart that cares and is committed to doing it the way that is right, the way that is true, the way that is beneficial for everybody that is involved combined with a sense of the strategy, planning, execution, and needs of the business. Then it is win, win, win. When a leader can do that they have the discernment to make good decisions.

What are some aspects of the Character, Relationships, Skills attributes important for a Servant Heart, Business Mind approach?

Character

→ Actively engage in the tension between compassion and outcomes, showing restraint where it's needed on either side because of the reality that exists.

Relationships

→ Foster dialogues and conversations that identify the business needs that support the long-term vision, while communicating with care, especially difficult decisions and actions.

Skills

→ Know your key business metrics, what drives success, and continuously assess and grow in areas the business needs.

Download an overview of the Character, Relationships, Skills aspects from all the Myths, and see them all in one place, by visiting www.redefineyourservantleadership.com.

A WHOLE NEW REALITY

When we see things differently, we will try new things, and get different results. I hope you see servant leadership differently than when you started the book, and differently than when you started the Replace section. I am confident that at least ONE of the ten myths about servant leadership that need to be replaced resonated with you. Most likely, more than one. Just in case there is any doubt about trading People-Pleasing for Mission-Driven, Passive for Assertive, or any of the myths, I want to share the increase that comes when you embrace servant leadership.

We introduced the Hercules Hold earlier. I shared what happens if we release the tension and let the grip on one pillar pull us too far (perhaps the Misguided Servant pillar). Low tension diminishes integrity, influence, and impact. Instead of living on the left side as a Misguided Servant, or the right side as a Bad Boss, embrace the characteristics of servant leadership and hold the tension of being a Mission-Driven, Aware, Principled, Servant Hearted and Business Minded Servant Leader.

When you do, you create something completely new, you replace the old, and redefine what's possible for everyone involved because leading in the high tension that is servant leadership increases your integrity, influence, and impact.

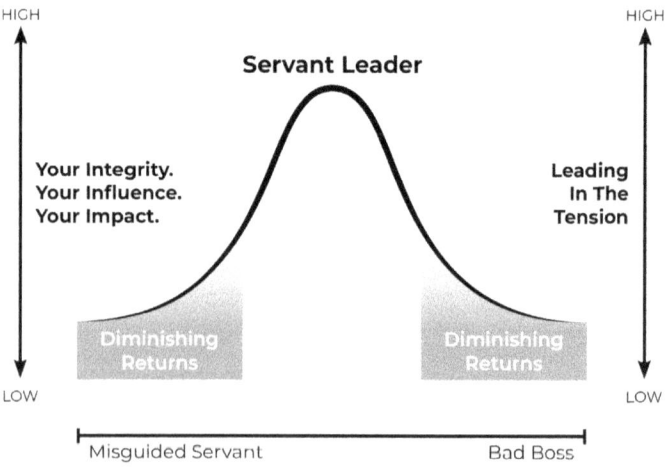

If there were a slider on the bottom line, it would be getting pulled to either side, and the effort the Servant Leader makes is to keep it in the middle. That is where the most tension will be as you challenge yourself not to slip too far towards being a Misguided Servant or a Bad Boss. Too far left or right is represented in those gray areas of diminishing return where you actually start to act against what you are trying to achieve — like we saw with the myths. In the middle, as the tension rises, the better you hold to servant leadership, so too rises your integrity, influence, and impact. This puts the Servant Leader right at the top of the bell curve in this diagram.

Let's look at Myth# 1 as an example: Servant Leaders are People-Pleasers. The more (and more) you please people, keep the peace, and make sure everyone is happy, the more you diminish your integrity. Because when you do, you now tell people only what they want to hear, which decreases their respect for you and your influence with them, and you feel you can't address performance issues and that erodes your impact as a leader.

On the flip side, truly Self-Serving Bad Bosses will place their desires over what the mission requires, take what they can first, and view their "subordinates" primary role as serving them — the boss. This decreases the team's passion and increases turnover, leaving them thinking they're being taken advantage of, and so they give minimum effort and request maximum compensation, and eventually resent authority while actively working against the Bad Boss.

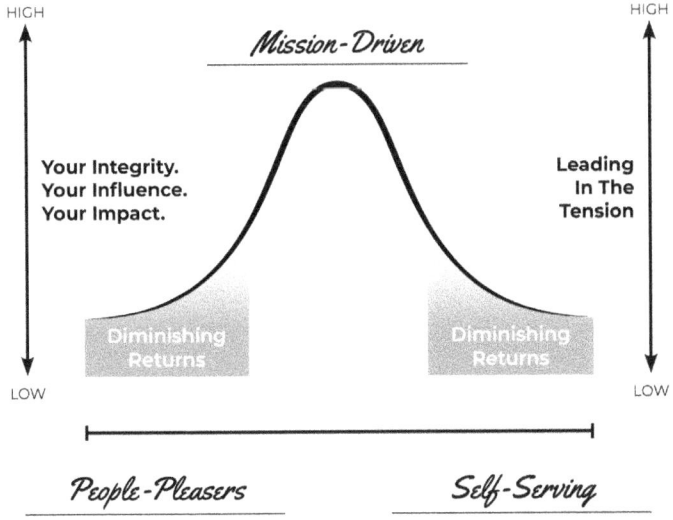

And finally, with a Mission-Driven approach by a Servant Leader who is holding the tension everything increases. Because the mission matters so much and deserves the best, you work to make peace, even through difficult conversations. You place the mission first, even above your own wishes, and because of that, others' respect for you grows. Because you serve people, honor them, and aim to help them grow, your influence grows. This shared purpose and mutually beneficial service fuels passion and inspires new ideas, the sacrifice for long hours and hard work, and an alignment that makes the business grow faster, and more effectively than before — ultimately amplifying your impact.

There is one myth that resonated with you more than the others. One that stuck out as a particularly challenging one for you to embrace with this new idea about servant leadership. Below this paragraph there is a blank diagram. Write that myth in the blanks. Take a moment to reflect on it. Write some of the outcomes you experience. Write down what might be possible when you embrace the tension of servant leadership. Is it time to embrace a new reality?

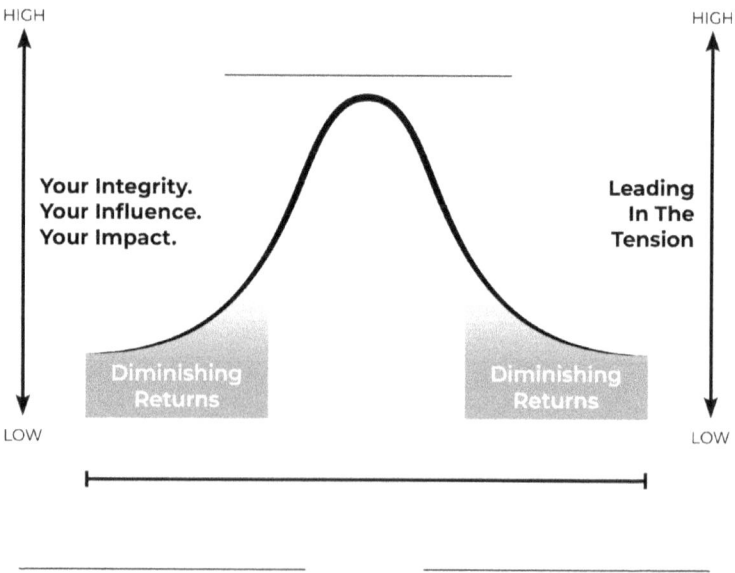

To download the diagram, visit www.redefineyourservantleadership.com.

Pick out another one. Write it out. Think about that. You can do it right now, or you can come back to it when you experience the myth in real life. The more you lead in the tension the greater your integrity, influence and impact will become.

Trying new things is no doubt challenging. Leading in the tension takes strength. Stamina. Resolve. Support. And so much more. In the rest of the book we're going to outline how to reinforce your growth and amplify your servant leadership.

REINFORCE

Can one tiny change transform your life? It's unlikely you would say so. But what if you made another? And another? And another?

Success is not a goal to reach or a finish line to cross. It is a system to improve, an endless process to refine.

The secret to getting results that last is to never stop making improvements.

— *Atomic Habits* by James Clear[24]

We have redefined servant Leadership, we have replaced myths that do not serve, and now it's time to reinforce your growth and success. In the last section, we went through ten ways to lead in the creative tension that produces the most integrity, most influence, and most impact. We talked about the Hercules Hold and what happens if we release one of the pillars. If you do not reinforce what you learn, what you learn will never take root. If you do not reinforce this growth in yourself, with the help of others, and through the actions you take, the change you hope to see will never sprout up or will quickly sprout up and die off.

Change is hard. It can be hard to plant it in our lives, have it take root, and grow. I find it can be hard to plant trees too. A few years ago, we were visiting my in-laws in the Hill Country in Texas, and they wanted to plant a tree. While the tree they wanted to plant was not native, it had the potential to thrive. We brought it to the house, dug the hole, planted the tree and watered the tree. Then, my in-laws went to Michigan for six months, like they always do. You know what happened to that tree? It died. It never took root. The elements and the animals ate that tree alive.

Good thing failure isn't final and you can always replant trees. Next year, we planted the same type of tree again. We planted it in almost the exact same location too. But this time, we planted it earlier in the season when the climate was friendlier and there was more time to water it before they left for Michigan. We also put anchors on four sides to keep it upright. Not wanting to take any chances we also built a protective (okay, semi-protective) fence around the tree with posts and chicken wire to keep the animals from demolishing it before it could stand on its own. My family and I also visited their house twice in the summer, and while there, we watered the tree and checked the fence. What do you think happened to this tree? The tree was taller, thicker, and had little green leaves on the branches. Fast forward five years, that same tree is thriving. No more fence and not as much watering from us. The tree is strong enough to withstand the often harsh climate, and tall enough with enough leaves to produce shade and offer relief from the Texas sun.

Our growth is very similar. Without the right elements, the nutrients, the right structure, the changes we try to make will not take root and they will be short lived. When I first began this process of redefining, like the first tree we planted, I immediately threw myself into challenging situations where the stakes were high and tried to set boundaries, engage in conflict, and make huge and challenging servant hearted business decisions. I failed. And I learned. I learned this work must first begin in me and how I see myself. I learned there needs to be relational and structural support to guide and nurture the growth, and I learned (or was painfully reminded) that new Skills take practice before you can be successful. What we do, especially when new, needs to be reinforced to support the growth and maturation process so new ideas and practices can take root and be strong enough to stand up to the pressures we face.

The great news is that in this book we've already talked about all the elements we need — identity, relationships, and practices. Now, let's add some ways for you to reinforce these new principles and practices in you, with others, and through some structure that supports the growth process to produce even greater integrity, influence, and impact in and through you.

As we begin, don't jump off the deep end like I did, but start slowly and take small steps as we outline them in each chapter of this section. If you never plant the tree there won't be anything to water, to anchor, or receive from in the future. There is a huge temptation to read something, think we've got it, but really leave with a social media "meme" level knowledge and application. I know, I've done it. Don't do that. Make the time you've already invested pay dividends for years by doing the work. On the flip side, there is a pull to do all the *me* work first. Let me get this all right in my head and my heart *before* I start trying new things with my team or sharing where I am struggling and need help. The truth is the growth happens when you go to people for what you need and by trying new things. In and through that process you reinforce the *me* work. Identity, relationships, and actions are all interconnected. These three parts reinforce each other, as they also reinforce growth and success. So, let's begin.

I AM A SERVANT LEADER

In his book, *Atomic Habits,* James Clear shows us that identity-based habits are a powerful (and effective) approach to ultimately change the outcomes we experience and the success we achieve. He says it begins with identifying who you wish to become, and that once you grasp who you want to become you can start taking steps to reinforce that identity. For many of us, this worked against the outcomes we experienced as servant leaders.[24]

- → I'm a People-Pleaser.
- → I'm no good at conflict.
- → I can't say no.
- → I'm no good with finance.
- → And countless more

Now it's time to flip it. To use the same power of identity to positively impact who we wish to be and how we act.

First, decide who you want to be as a leader. While outlining aspects of an identity for servant leaders has been a focus of this book, it is up to you to choose who you want to be as a leader. You need to begin by answering big, and foundational, questions: How do you define leadership? What is your mission in life and leadership? What are your principles and values? Who, and how, do you wish to be as a leader? It may produce thoughts and identity statements like this:

→ I choose to serve the mission first and people always in a kind and compassionate way.

→ I am the type of person who serves great needs with each no, and yes, I choose.

→ I am the type of leader who engages in conflict to strengthen relationships and improve outcomes.

→ I am the type of person who combines the heart and mind to make wise business and people decisions.

Take the time to reflect, to write, and then refine your identity as a servant leader. When you find yourself believing, or saying, something that runs counter to who you want to be as a leader examine it and redefine it. Let these aspects of your identity as a leader lead you — your mission, values, beliefs, and actions that align with your Character — not those of others. You will find tremendous peace, confidence, and a new found drive to reinforce that identity through what you do.

SMALL, SMART STEPS SERVE WELL

I shared with you that I dove straight into high stakes, challenging situations. I also shared I failed. These failures led me to question my growing identity as a leader. Can I really do this? Is this who I am and how I want to be? Sometimes diving into the deep end is required, but the preferred approach is to start small, where the stakes are low and the challenge is manageable. Repeated small, smart actions will produce progress, and it is the progress that produces dramatic change over time.

What small step can you take today?

I can't tell you how many times I've asked this question, or a variation of it, in coaching. We see grand gestures and dramatic changes portrayed instantaneously in movies, the news, everywhere. We believe, and kind of wish, it was like Steve Rogers turning into Captain America instantaneously and immediately jumping into the action. The trouble, beyond that not being reality, is when we do not yet have the competence to meet the challenge we become afraid. If that fear is too great, we freeze or forget it altogether. Look for small steps like:

→ Schedule the meeting you know is needed, but avoid

→ Leaving (or putting away work) at a specific time

→ Telling the Kind Truth to a trusted colleague

→ Saying "That doesn't work for me"

Each action, no matter how small, toward your identity and goals reinforces who you are and contributes to your growth. These small steps are what produce the skills that deliver the results that create momentum and grow your confidence. We started with who you wish to be. Now that we are also taking small steps and making progress, let's be *smart* about it and aim these actions specifically at goals that reinforce your identity and produce the results you hope for.

Zig Ziglar said, *"If you aim at nothing, you will hit it every time."* [18] We aren't aiming at nothing, but we aren't dialed in yet. Aiming at something specific is smart. Aiming at something is as simple as setting goals. Goals are how we identify the growth we hope to achieve, they guide how we will achieve it, and give us the feedback we need to know if we did or not. That is smart. You gain the clarity, guidance, and ability to measure success when your goals are specific, measurable, actionable, realistic, and time-bound. Here are the criteria for each component of *SMART* goals:

→ Specific: Make your goal focused and detailed, not vague and general.

→ Measurable: Clarify the criteria for success so you can monitor progress, celebrate milestones, and evaluate if you achieved your goal.

→ Actionable: Use action verbs to describe what you will do to grow and achieve the goal.

→ Realistic: This does not mean easy — it means it is possible through intentional actions over time. Goals can, and should, be a little risky and stretch us.

→ Time-bound: Designate a specific time frame or deadline by when you will achieve the goal.

The goal of *SMART* goals isn't to complicate it. It is to structure your growth and aim it where you intend it to go. Don't get caught up in perfectly completing the goal formula only to lose your goal — or worse, your desire to work on your goal. This goal methodology serves you, not the other way around. So, use it to add the structure you need, but keep it simple so it is useful. Big, confusing, or flowery words complicate our understanding. This goal is for you, not the newspaper. Write it in a way you can understand it, so you can (and will) continue to act on it. The work is hard enough, keep everything that supports your work simple. On the following page are a few examples to get you started.

→ Kindly, disagree with an individual or an idea at least ONCE per week for six months. *(A real goal of mine seven years ago)*

→ Delegate three projects and five key responsibilities to Amy and Joe by August 31 of this year.*

→ Build my "Personal Leadership Team" by the end of this month.*

→ Grow my departments' net profit margin by December 31st of this year by ending X program and increase sales through Y service.*

These were intentionally left semi-vague for the sake of when you read this book. When you write your goal, write the specific date — day, month, year. Also, please do choose someone else if you don't know an Amy or Joe.

Write your first goal right now. Take out your journal, a piece of paper, or simply write in the margin of this book. You may write more than one. *To download a goal template, visit www.redefineyourservantleadership.com.*

And now you're thinking, how many do I need? I don't think there is a magic number. Trust your gut. My growth value, when unchecked, means I will write nine goals for nine different areas of my life, that outline the next fifteen years of my life. Then I promptly stop doing everything. It's too much. I found I can handle about three written, high priority goals at a time. Your number may be different, It doesn't mean I (or you) am not working on growing in other aspects of life. It simply means there is extra focus, effort, and time given to the important goals in that season.

Even with clear goals, small steps, and clearly knowing who (and how) you want to be as a leader you could still fail. In fact, if you do it alone — you will. We said "it is lonely at the top" is a terrible leadership mantra, and working on your goals alone is a recipe for failure. Growth doesn't happen in isolation — it happens in Relationships. Yes, you need to (and will grow) by practicing and working these things out in real time, in a real setting, around real people. But also, you grow in, with, and through real Relationships. To truly reinforce your identity and growth as a leader you need to use your people.

USE YOUR PEOPLE

Use your people? Are you sure? Of course we are not talking about abusing, merely getting what you want, or carelessly discarding people once you're through with them. That's awful. We said earlier healthy Relationships are mutually beneficial. It is a connection where each person can serve the other, AND be served. Like our tree which needed help from outside itself to receive support and water, it is in and through Relationships that we are able to receive all five of the aspects of healthy Relationships. We need things if we are going to grow, succeed, and thrive. They are people who are:

- → For us
- → Present
- → Give encouragement
- → Speak truth
- → Call to act

Each one of these elements are needed, by each of us, at various times in life, (heck, throughout the day) and especially leadership and seasons of growth and change. This is why your Personal Leadership Team (coach, mentor, friend, cheerleader, and partner) is so vital to your success. One, because no one person can give you all you need at any one time. And two, because there is more wisdom, experience, perspective, and shared knowledge to gain through multiple people than just one. At Leadwell we believe in the power of training + application + Relationships so much we build our programs with practice in mind. We set up six or twelve months of coaching with individuals or groups as a part of our leadership development programs. We bring together information, application-based growth, making sure that you continuously get the feedback loops, and the opportunity to practice, test ideas, and deepen Relationships to increase peer support in and after a program finishes.

Now that you know what you need, who your people are, and what growth goal you're working towards it is up to you to ask for what you need. I get it, it's awkward for all of us. We may have to swallow our pride a bit, show we don't have it all together, use "weird" ooey-gooey language, or just do something we've never done because *we* are the giver. Here's something that helped me internalize the idea that it is okay to receive. If you don't ask for what you need you rob the other person of the opportunity to serve you. Here are a few ways to ask for what you need from people to reinforce your growth.

→ I am setting new boundaries at work, can you help keep me accountable to them and ask me how it's going?

→ I need to get something off my chest, can you listen without judging me or telling someone else?

→ I'm trying to make a good decision in a tough situation, can you give me some advice?

→ It's been a tough week. I need a little pick-me-up. Can you give me encouragement or motivation to keep going?

→ Will you share feedback about how I am coming off to others after this meeting?

It sounds weird, I know. You don't want to burden people. Remember, these are people who are *for* you. They want you to win, and helping you is a way they can serve. If they can't or won't they have permission to say no. If they say, when it's all said and done, ask them how it felt who you asked for their support. My guess is you will hear answers like honored, valued, and needed. Not that I felt obligated. Healthy Relationships and healthy people. Growing Relationships and growing people are NOT a burden, they are a blessing.

You need to give yourself permission to focus on yourself. By asking for help or by dedicating time and energy to your growth. You are living into a new identity, applying new information, working out ideas and behaviors, new Skills, approaches, and working toward a goal. You need to focus on yourself and your growth. Like the tension, this isn't a 100% of the time focus. It is an intentional focus for a period of the day or season in life. And, those help and reinforcement you are requesting doesn't demand 100% of their time or attention either. This focus isn't just reflection and having people "look at" or help you. This focus includes intentional practice, in a real setting, that produces real growth.

We need to *reinforce the growth* and maturation process.

So new ideas and practices can take root and be strong enough *to stand up to the pressures we face.*

Keep trying new skills. Maybe you try communication and find you are good at it and your pace accelerates. But then you are working on discernment and you go one step forward and two steps back. You need time to work through all the different areas where you want to grow. This is where most people get stuck. People don't commit over time. If you're an athlete, the growing stage is the practice that you're doing outside of practice because you want to perform better than everybody else. It's the after hours free throws. It's getting to the pool at four in the morning to get your laps in before you start work. If you're writing a book it looks like putting more words down than you might need because you know editing is going to take time.

I can't stress enough, you need practice, and you need loads and loads of practice. I'm not saying that the way that they prepare doctors is the best way, but the way that they prepare doctors through residency and internship and medical school is a tremendous amount of repetition in a very short period of time. They know that with repetition, and with repetition in more kinds of scenarios, you become even better and more responsive even in the unknown.

You also need grace and truth. You're not going to get anything right straight out of the gate. I thought because of who I am and how smart I am, that I was going to get it right. I thought things would go the way I thought they were gonna go the very first time I did it, and I was going to get the same results as the individual who had been doing it that way for over 30 years. And the truth is, that's not going to happen. It didn't happen for me, and it's not going to happen for you. You need grace to figure it out as you go and to get better as you go. You also need truth. Truth looks like proper information. Truth is feedback, feedback from the outside, from another individual, from somebody that can give you an impression of what worked and what didn't. Coaches can do this — and I often am privileged to be in this position with clients where I am a mirror for them or a trusted truth teller.

Finally, teaching is a great way to keep moving forward. One of the best ways to sustain your growth and cement your learning is to teach others. When you do, you cement the ideas and actions for yourself, as a part of your Character, and you work them out even deeper because you need to be able to communicate not just what, but how.

Take the experiences you've gone through. The lessons you learned in this book and throughout your leadership journey and turn around and be a coach, a mentor, a cheerleader, or a friend to somebody else. This is the mutually beneficial Relationship with your Personal Leadership Team, yes, but also with those you work with and who follow you. Each of us need each other to better each other. Use your people and serve your people. Teach what you learned, to serve. When you teach you create a legacy of leadership. That is one way to amplify this growth in you — and beyond you.

The other ways to amplify your servant leadership are through *consistency* and *intensity*. That first could look like consistently leading and living for years, a lifetime even, continuously redefining your servant leadership and growing to meet the needs of the mission and the people. The second is to amplify your servant leadership by increasing the intensity. To go further up and further into the idea of servant leadership, to your values and beliefs, seeking to remove whatever gets in the way of what you hope to accomplish.

If you want to see what a lifetime of impact as a servant leader could look like. This next section is for you.

Do you have a life-giving, world-changing vision so big that the only way it might be possible is if you go all in?

This next section is for you.

AMPLIFY

One cannot tiptoe around the edge hoping to change themselves, let alone the world. They must go all in. Go all in on that which is good, and right, and life-giving. They must give up. Give up that which gets in the way of what they seek to accomplish. They must see what's possible through them, when it doesn't all have to come to them. When one does they redefine it all and might just change themselves, and the world.

— With encouragement, Jon

In the last section, we talked about reinforcing our new definitions and the myths we replaced about servant leadership. You've likely started demonstrating your Character by testing what it's like to respectfully disagree with someone in authority, assert your needs, or communicate more clearly and candidly. When you did, you experienced a new found respect for yourself, and you saw others' respect for you grow too.

You may also feel your influence growing, you have greater confidence in making business decisions with a servant heart, and even with what you've done so far you are experiencing better results and a greater impact.

This book is packed full of information. You've worked through some of the sections up to this point, and are embracing servant leadership and your identity as a servant leader. Keeping leaning into those ideas. Keep taking on new parts of the book as they feed your leadership needs. Consistency will amplify your impact. Keep growing. Growth is essential, because change is inevitable.

This section will dive even deeper into the power of holding the tension in servant leadership. Read it, take what you want, and continue to come back for further growth ideas and areas, examples, and encouragement.

Ready to double-down? Do things others wouldn't do? To achieve something that might just be impossible, but will amplify your impact to another level? This section will show what you need to do. Here's the first tension you can live into to level up.

To level up, you must give up.

GIVE UP

I bet you didn't expect that header. Give up. I urge a relentless optimism, and now I tell you to give up. Relentless optimists never give up (agreed!). I am not saying give up on leadership, that's not what we're talking about. I am talking about giving up the things that get in the way of your leadership.

Giving up is truly where servant leaders amplify their leadership. Let me explain. We said leadership is *the act of influencing the attitude, thoughts, and behaviors of others toward a shared purpose.* If you have found that definition of servant leadership works for you and have seen a little of the impact, you are ready to know the power behind the definition. What servant leaders are doing when they put the shared purpose first is they are willfully giving up their own ego. Yes, there is pleasure in success, and a feeling of gratification when a team or an organization absolutely kills it. But it is not about the personal standing of the leader. Servant leaders amplify their integrity, influence, and impact when they *willfully give up personal standing* for the sake of the purpose, people, and places they lead. Here is the amplified definition of servant leadership, in its entirety:

Servant leadership is the act of influencing the attitudes, thoughts, and behaviors of others toward a shared purpose *by willfully giving up personal standing*.

What is personal standing? Personal standing is a thing or quality that belongs or relates to one particular person rather than to other people. Since it is a thing or quality you possess you also get to choose what you do with it and how you use it. It is at your disposal, a tool, to be used for good, for evil, for personal use, or to serve others. What aspects of a leader's personal standing most often get in the way of what they hope to accomplish?

Pride. Power. Position. Possessions.

These four are not an exhaustive list, but they are a critical list. When you give up these four aspects of personal standing — pride, power, position, and possessions — you remove much of what limits a leader's ability to be impactful.

In our world it is pride, power, personal status or our position at work, profits (all money really), and possessions that too often get in the way. They get in the way of our desired (and portrayed) Character, in the way of our Relationships, and in the way of the actual work. They distort our view of reality, of what's really important. We believe lies about what we must do. As a result we do things to protect this personal standing and chase after unfulfilling and unattainable ideals and goals. Giving up personal standing is so foreign to us because we get trained and taught and shown that you've got to be the one at the top and that powerful people will prevail. The reality is that none of that helps leaders lead well.

We gained leadership strength by replacing myths with the proper tension of a servant leader, which results in a stronger, truer Character, deeper, healthier Relationships, and permission to use your Skills to serve the business and the people. And the same will happen when giving up personal standing and replacing the myth about how important it is. The result will be an amplification of your integrity, influence, and impact because you show everyone where your true priorities lie.

What you have done is you've shown that what you say you serve is actually more important than some of the ways the world keeps score about what you do or who you are. You show you measure success by fulfilling the mission you are on through serving the needs of others, and leading them to succeed. Through the process of giving up, you may also just change the world.

Let's take these aspects one at a time.

Pride

Pride is a leadership cancer. And like cancer it is hard to put your finger on, it hides, and it metastasizes. It is THE one that overtly or covertly, influences all other aspects of your life and leadership. Pride, the need for the focus to be on you, about you and what you've done, only grows the more you feed it. Pride will cause us to place perception and appearance above our actual Character, impacting our integrity. Pride hinders our Relationships, keeping everybody at arm's length because we fear being found out when we get too close, and because others dislike self-promotion, whether it is overt or covert. You know, that self-deprecating type of pride that too often portrays a false sense of humility while truly seeking to be seen.

Pride never allows us to choose the *mission first, people always* approach. It will force us to people-please and serve ourselves, to be always available or unapproachable because of how we are seen in the process. When pride is present we must either avoid power or seek power because in both cases we are the focus of the action. Pride, like cancer, must be removed, completely. The other three aspects — power, position, possessions — we share and we use with and for others. Pride is one that must be given up, and continually given up otherwise it will continue to spread and infect you, the people around you, and where you lead. What are powerful antidotes for pride? Humility and gratitude.

As we found when we dug into humility earlier, a summary of what C.S. Lewis said is that, "[...] *humility is not thinking less of ourselves; it is thinking of ourselves less.*" [21] As a leader, give of yourself in the service of others. Because you have a calling that is greater than you, you can humble yourself, making the focus of your efforts that mission — the work — and the beneficiary the people and the place(s) you serve. As the focus on you decreases, your impact through your work increases — it's amplified. When this happens you will realize the freedom that comes to lead and serve as needed when you don't have to be the focus.

Gratitude also frees us from the prison of pride. Gratitude requires us to look beyond ourselves and what we've done. Think quickly about all the help you receive right now — from family, coworkers, business partners, even the government and those people who help promote your work by sharing on social media. Now, think about all the help you received in starting your business, getting the promotion, being developed as a leader, even the person or Amazon driver who gave you this book. We immediately see the contributions others make and how much we rely on each other, how we've been given, not earned. Because of this, we are compelled to be grateful. The most natural response is to be grateful. It also helps solidify that right sized view of ourselves in relation to the work that's done and the world around us. When pride creeps up, look around at all there is to see and how much happens without you — often despite you — and be grateful.

When pride is put to death, the ability to give up power, position, and possessions becomes possible.

Power

We talked about power in Myth #9. In that section, we replaced the myth that a servant leader must avoid power (that's a misguided servant) and instead explored that servant leaders share power responsibly. Go back and take a look if this does not ring a bell. We talked about empowering people — giving power to another. It's not exactly a huge surprise that it is in the *Give Up* chapter. Let's dive deeper and see what happens when we go beyond sharing power to giving up power, specifically when you empower others and choose to use your earned influence.

First, let's squash any thought of us talking about "giving away your power" in a psychological sense where you give away your power and are controlled by another, or believe your feelings, thoughts, or actions don't matter. We've already said servant leaders share power and are assertive. We're not talking about giving it away by losing your temper, getting defensive, or being intimidated. No, we are talking about the authority or power you gain as a leader to impact decisions, direction, and the lives of others.

George Washington, the first president of the United States, had the power to make a decision that would've changed the direction of all of our lives. After two terms as president, people wanted him to run again. Heck, they actually tried to make him king, but he already turned that down. In the face of certain victory and an ever increasing power in a blossoming nation George Washington declined to run again because he believed the country was strong enough to withstand a change in leadership, and that this change in leadership was best long term for the new nation. The influence of his decision led other presidents to honor this tradition, without rule or law, for 144 years until Franklin D. Roosevelt began his third term in office in 1941, in the middle of World War II.

Choose influence over power. That is the earning of respect, credibility, your ability to affect the circumstance because your Character, Relationships, and Skills — not power — you gain their hearts, not just their actions. A leader with power can say, "Because I said so" to get people to do as they wish. Power can drive action, but influence fuels inspiration. The restraint of using power for personal gain or using power to uplift others is attractive and reinforces where your priorities truly lie. Using well-earned influence moves people further along towards a shared purpose because you move their hearts.

When leaders use earned influence and not power, people give more than the time they are paid to work, they use their full selves. This act of sacrificial empowerment actually inspires people to work harder, faster, longer. While frustrating and sometimes a slower process, especially in the beginning, you will find that in the long run choosing influence, and giving up lead with power, produce more stable, lasting results and creates a more powerful environment where all can (and will) contribute.

Position

Giving up your position doesn't look like stepping down, it looks like stepping into using your title, status, or privilege in ways people don't expect. We expect people to use their position to get their way, increase their status, and create distance between themselves and other people. Instead of the position serving you, when you give up the position, you use it to help advance the mission, create connections, and improve the lives of others. When position isn't something you get, but something you give (and use) you create opportunities to serve that wouldn't otherwise be possible.

Leaders often have platforms because of their position. If they call a meeting, people come. When they speak, people listen. It could be in their company, in government, on social media, or from an actual platform — like a stage. Or a pulpit. Gregg Matte is pastor at Houston's First Baptist Church in Houston, TX. His leadership, especially his integrity and influence, has earned him a fairly large platform.

Each week he preaches to thousands or tens of thousands. Regularly he offers council to city and local leaders. He's thrown the first pitch at an Astros game and led the NFL's Houston Texans in chapel multiple times. He even served as campaign chaplain for a presidential candidate. Where some may use this to grow their platform, Gregg uses this to grow the work he is called to and people, especially those in need. Because of his position he could be distant and comfortable, instead he goes out of his way to connect, to make others feel comfortable, and to serve in challenging places all around the world. He advocates on behalf of churches, not just his church. Through his position, Gregg will champion the needs of the poor, the widow, the orphan, to name a few. As Gregg's platform grows so do his invitations to pastors, especially pastors who are a different race than him, from different countries than him, who don't have the reach Gregg does. He invites them to preach from his platform to extend their reach, and the collective impact of the work they do.

Giving up your position doesn't necessarily mean you avoid the exclusive groups, the status, and the "Leader Only" invites. These may be some of the key places you have to influence others toward your cause and to why and how you lead. Instead, in all circumstances use your position to help the position of the work you do (your mission), the people who work with you, and the people you serve. Where positions often create distance, use yours to drive connection and demonstrate no person or job is lesser or not needed. When you do you amplify your values, mission, and create a healthier, more resilient, and service-oriented environment for all involved. Give up the ability to avoid and distance yourself that comes with a leadership position and you will gain the ability to influence and impact what's needed most.

Possessions

Giving up your possessions as a leader can sound trite, like suggesting that you give away your corner office or your car or your favorite coffee mug at work. That's great, we shouldn't hesitate to do those good things, but it is not what I'm getting at.

Servant leaders amplify their integrity, influence, and impact when they *willfully give up personal standing* for the sake of the purpose, people, and places they lead.

Giving up your possessions completely can be good, and perhaps needed. Giving them up also looks like sharing what you have in service to others. Sharing the abundance, showcases your heart for the work and your love for the people providing inspiration and an example to follow. Servant leaders who give up their possessions have a *through, not to* mentality. Servant leaders see what is produced — profits, rewards, even entire businesses — as something to be stewarded. They are not the end of the line but another party who gets to enjoy the process. They also get to share to amplify what they care about most.

Through, not to may look like an organization profit sharing with their employees. It may look like a human trafficking awareness organization using their platforms and distributing funds to other human trafficking organizations doing the work behind the scenes. It may look like investment in research, training, market development — whatever investment might be needed to produce a return for the people and work you do — to be of even greater service moving forward.

We all have various levels of possessions — personally and professionally. You could share tools and equipment, resources, and workspaces. Personal material possessions that can be given in service could be cars, homes, property, clothes, and much more. And personally, we have intangibles we possess like our time, attitude, thoughts, and actions. Turning around and using those possessions — whether they are personal or organizational — to further your shared purpose creates an even greater impact. Creating an exhaustive list is impossible. Instead, let's look at when giving up a possession might be for everyone's best interest.

You can ask yourself: Do I have my possessions or do my possessions have me?

If your possessions have you — you will fight, hoard, and work to keep them and get more of them. If you have them — they can (and should) be enjoyed, but each possession also becomes a resource at your disposal to serve people and advance the mission.

How might *through, not to* amplify the way you use money? How might sharing personal possessions, professional resources, or your platform, communicate what's most important? If we look at ourselves, our organizations, anything we do with a *through, not to* mentality, then we can make a larger impact than we ever could alone.**

Through, not to is a great mindset for servant leaders, yes. In fact, it is a critical step in amplifying our servant leadership — and the impact of the work we do. As long as we see it as *to* us, not *through* us we cannot give up what gets in the way and go all in on what's needed.

***Through, not to is another place to hold the tension. It doesn't mean if you do NOT give up all your worldly possessions, refuse to take a promotion, or make more money you are somehow NOT a servant leader. Or, if you do, you are holier than others. I hope you do not feel judged — personally or organizationally — that is not in my heart, nor is it the intent. The intent is to highlight another way, to bring about reflection, and to see all that we have as a means for serving. And maybe, just maybe, not out of guilt — but out of a joy-filled, generous spirit — we make a difference in this world we never thought possible.*

IT'S THE BARNHARTS

It was August 2022. A Friday. The Friday of the first week the kids were back in school. And at 8:30 p.m., no less. Normally, Meghan and I would be unwinding and recovering. But on this night we were on a Zoom call. A pastor at our church, Brad, kept touting this guy Alan Barnhart. When he asked us to register he kept saying, "It's the Barnharts," like that meant something to us. Which it didn't at the time. Little did I know that brief Zoom call with the Barnharts would further redefine and amplify my view of servant leadership and forever impact my family, life, and business.

Supposedly, this couple, Alan and Katherine Barnhart, were business owners with a strong marriage and a generous approach to philanthropy, so we gave our exhausted Friday night to the Zoom call. Imagine, Meghan and I are sitting on the couch, we've got Zoom open, some popcorn and sparkling water. We're ready.

We expected a bit of pomp and circumstance for the event. Turns out Alan was sick, so he was in the basement of his house. A typical Midwest, middle-class basement with a comfy recliner and a screen window full of bugs. His wife, Katherine was upstairs on an iPhone. We immediately got the impression that these were two of the most unassuming, humble people that you'll likely ever meet. Honestly, I began to feel a bit dismayed. I thought the Zoom event might turn out to be a bit underwhelming and underdeliver on my expectations. Boy, was I wrong.

Alan took over as CEO of his family's crane and rigging company in the 1980s. When they did, he and his wife Katherine, along with his brother made the choice to do business a bit differently. Alan and Katherine chose to live on a fixed income, less than one might assume for a CEO. They chose to live on the average salary of a middle-class family in Memphis, where they lived. And this couple was living modestly, not for a CEO, for anyone. Which was fine — it emphasized their values for sure. It was not all that remarkable until Alan shared the annual gross revenue of the business and the impact they were making around the world.

That year Barnhart Crane and Rigging was a $500 MILLION business! But wait for it… Beyond living modestly and having a thriving business, they give generously. Not just a little bit more generously. I mean outrageously generous. They gave away $35 million! That year! They reinvest half of their profits in the business and give the other HALF away.

This was a kind of servant leadership that made me — made us — very curious, and encouraged us about what might be possible when a servant heart and business mind get pointed at and devoted to a good, right, and life-giving mission that drives everything.

At this point I sat up on the couch. I realized this wasn't a couple who does it a little differently with a little better results. This was something completely different, and as a result of them going all in, they amplified the business, their philanthropy and the lives of people around the world. I had to learn more. I went all in to attempt to learn how the Barnharts amplified their servant leadership, and how I (and others) could do the same.

Here is what I learned about the Barnharts' radical and life-changing example of giving up what was getting in the way of what they wanted to achieve. It can serve as a model for us to amplify our servant leadership beyond ourselves and truly go all in — in life, in business, wherever we lead.

They lead by example, yes, through a humble approach, modest lifestyle, mission-driven, and gently assertive approach to what they believe and the mission they are on. On top of their personal example, it's baked into the business that is Barnhart Crane and Rigging. Take some time to review the below purpose, mission, and core values. Look specifically for the redefined servant leadership aspects like mission-driven, principled, assertive, empowering, and servant heart, business mind.

PURPOSE STATEMENT

The purpose of Barnhart is to glorify God by developing people and encouraging them to use their skills and gifts in His service through constructive work, personal witness and ministry funding.

MISSION STATEMENT

Barnhart Crane and Rigging Co. will continuously improve and grow to be the best in our industry.[25]

CORE VALUES

→ **Safety** — We invest the necessary resources to ensure safe operations.

→ **Servant Leadership** — We serve our people by providing purpose, trust, belonging, progress, recognition and compensation.

→ **Quality Service** — We develop our people and processes to ensure consistent service and operational excellence to meet the needs of our customers.

→ **Innovation** — We create better methods and tools to meet the needs of our customers.

→ **Continuous Improvement** — We evaluate every aspect of our company in order to improve.

→ **Fairness** — We are honest and fair to our people, vendors and customers.

→ **Profit with a Purpose** — We work to make profit and invest the profit to reward our teams, grow the company and meet the needs of people locally and globally.[25]

I had the privilege of interviewing Alan in preparation for writing this book. During the interview, I asked him about the dichotomy between profit and purpose, people and performance. I shared how some people saw those as mutually exclusive. He paused. Then, he stated they are not mutually exclusive, they are complementary. To him purpose and profit, people and performance reinforce one another, and make the other even stronger. I grinned. I realized in that moment the wholeness and strength that leading, over a lifetime, in the tension of serving and leading, devoting one's self to something greater than themself, and striving to grow and empower others redefines you completely, sets you apart, and is the path to unfathomably amplifying your impact.

What do those amplified results look like you ask?

→ In 2021 Barnhart Crane and Rigging was a $430 million dollar business that donated $35 million dollars in one year.

→ At the time of my research, Barnhart was roughly a $600 million business and anticipated donating $50 million dollars in one year.

→ According to LinkedIn, the median tenure of employees at Barnhart was 6.2 years. (Average is 4.1 and dropping)[26]

→ Glassdoor listed the approval rating of the CEO (Alan) at 98%. (Average is 73%)[27]

You may think that is it, but it is truly the tip of the iceberg. Alan and Katherine, in service of something greater than themselves, humbled themselves and gave up what they believed would get in the way of their ultimate goal of glorifying God and funding His ministry.

→ Alan and Katherine chose a modest income, a middle-class income for Memphis families, and referenced never making more in a year than ~$150,000–$178,000, and some years even less. (Median income for CEO's according to Salary.com is $832,600)[28]

→ Instead of deciding for themselves where and what to give, they invite any team member (and their spouse) to be a part of the GROVE Group and vet, decide, and steward the donations they make.[29]

→ In 2007 the Barnharts gave 99% of the business to the National Christian Foundation and kept one percent of the voting and operating stock.

Yes, you read that right. At the time, they gave away a nearly $250 million dollar business.

→ In 2012 they went all in. They gave the *last* one percent away and now operate the business as trustees.

I mean, heck, if you're willing to give it up, you may as well go all in. But seriously, how unfathomable is all of that. It is a bit overwhelming too. There is no guilt or mandate that *you* must do all of it. That's not why I share this. I share this to show what may be possible if you choose to.

Alan and Katherine didn't share these details, the donations, any of it for years. Not even with their closest friends. When they started in the 1980s it wasn't what it is today. But, the foundation was set. They just needed to lean into the tension. Into what might be possible. I am grateful they choose to lean into life as servant leaders. I am grateful they chose to share their story. Their example amplifies their work and what's possible. It extends their impact beyond themselves.

They are an example to me, my wife, my family, and my business as we strive to replicate many of the principles and ideals the Barnharts demonstrate. Contentment, humility, service, generosity. One practical way, of the many, is that we share 50% of our profits each year. Another is going all in on the purpose, mission, and values of the business.

Where might you go all in?

GO ALL IN

If you're willing to give up, you may as well go all in. When we go all in on the things that matter most to who we are personally, or to our organization, they pay dividends, not only for us, but for others because we amplify and extend our service. Too often, we tiptoe around the edge believing the lie that if we make the focus too narrow, if we choose one thing over another, we will be giving up so many opportunities.

What Alan and Katherine did by going all in is open the door to their mission, principles, behaviors, company, and generosity positively changing their lives and the lives of their family, coworkers, company, and the world — forever. As a leader, you influence the attitude, thoughts, and behaviors of others toward a shared purpose. Go all in yourself as an example for others to follow. Go all in on that purpose, the principles, and values that guide and support it so those who are with you clearly know what to run toward.

We have a mission, but rarely review it or tie our work to it. We put core values on the wall, but never teach or correct based on what we see in the hall. The truth is, even when you think the keyhole is too small for any sort of impact to get through, when you go all in you open the door to a world of possibilities even greater than you imagined. Going all in ensures that the change you experience through redefining your servant leadership will change others' lives too.

What are some examples of what it might look like to go all in?

→ Hiring, promoting, firing to the core values instead of merely placing them on the wall

→ Giving a higher percentage of profits to causes that you care about

→ Creating enough margin in the budget to give some of your nonprofit's revenue to partner nonprofits on the same mission as yours

→ Giving earned (or paid) media opportunities to another organization

→ Using your personal standing to assert your beliefs about any area of injustice in the world

→ Incorporating a cause you care about — perhaps individuals with Special Needs — into the fabric of your business through employment and training

→ Sacrificing time, money, and effort to mobilize a group of people to serve or go on a mission trip (personally or professionally)

What might it look like for you to go all in?
What might be amplified when you do?

The more you go all in the more free you become to lead and to serve. The tension of leading and serving creates something completely new, stronger, and impactful — in you and through you. Going all in on that sacrifice makes you stronger, builds your ability to continue, and produces even greater Character, Relationships, and Skills in the process. The ripples of inspiration and impact leave a legacy of impact beyond what you will ever know. It resonates, it amplifies, and it creates an absolutely radical and life changing example for everyone else to follow.

You likely started reading this book because you were frustrated by the pressures, expectations, or results you were getting as a "servant leader." You wanted to be a more effective leader, more influential, and do it in a way where you were fulfilled. You discovered a new definition, the Character, Relationships, and Skills needed to lead well, and what to replace to lead with even greater integrity, influence, and impact, while reinforcing and amplifying your growth and impact. In the process you discovered a freedom you might not have believed to be possible.

I urge you to continue to find ways to give up and go all in on good things, because when you do, the impact on your life — and the world — is endless. As I move into the last section of the book, I want to tell you about a place I've gone all in and explain the life changing example that brought me to this understanding, and actually all the wisdom in the book.

REDEFINING IT ALL

Is faith something that is important to you?

If you've made it this far, you have a great deal of faith. Reading leadership books, getting an MBA, or attending trainings takes a tremendous amount of faith. They propose a different way of looking at things for the possibility of getting better results. It takes faith to say "What I just read or learned is going to work for me. I'm willing to give it a try (maybe even go all in)." It takes faith to change how you lead. To start having difficult conversations. To set boundaries. The entire act of leadership takes faith, you place your faith in people and that doing the right things will produce results. It is said about faith that faith is confidence in what we hope for and assurance about what we do not see. If you made it this far, I believe you are a person of great faith.

You've read my references to faith a handful of times throughout the book. Faith is important to me. Faith is a core value of mine, and I have faith in God. However, this faith in God, like my original view on servant leadership, was skewed. It was a surface level faith. It was focused on the motions, how it — I mean *I* — looked to others, and that I really had to work *really* hard to be "holy." You might be thinking yep — that's my understanding of it, too. Lots of impossible standards, things you can't do, and guilt when you get it wrong. That isn't really faith at all. My faith was based very little on my faith, it was based on the work I did to earn it.

What I discovered when I began digging into the Bible for my new definition of leadership blew me away. I had a view of God, and Jesus, that was pretty basic. Naive even. Like I said, I knew and tried to adhere to the high standards and holiness, but I saw Jesus as many good things, yes. I also saw Jesus as primarily meek, nice, subservient, passive, even permissive at times. In my digging-in I discovered that Jesus, way before Greenleaf's book in 1970, introduced (created) the idea of servant leadership. His life and example of servant leadership redefined the world at the time, and for all time.

Jesus modeled a gentle strength. In fact, his modeling is what I base my leadership on. It is what I base my own behavior on. It is how I know modeling works. In fact, when I am assessing the usefulness of my own work I make sure it is supported by biblically-based principles. Jesus was assertive with the truth, and gentle with people. He was kind always, and even when rebuking people he aimed to connect, to grow, and to give life to them. Jesus would pour himself out completely in service to God and to people, and then he would withdraw to connect with God, revisit what the mission required of him, and rest. He used his power to heal, to teach, and to save those in need. Jesus shared His power with those who follow Him and even told them they would do even greater things that He would. He exemplified perfect boundaries with people and by holding true to His values and principles while inviting any and all to join, and never settling for less but creating a way to meet His high standards. He respected the authority and power given to others and in doing so demonstrated what it looks like to lead without pride or position, generously sharing power and possessions. I think all of this will ring a bell and that is on purpose. These are the bedrock ideas and foundations of my work.

While our world isn't perfect, let's just look at the impact Jesus's teachings had on the world in a few ways by people imperfectly trying to do what he taught. The faith of Rosa Parks and Martin Luther King, Jr. in the teaching of Jesus that all people, of all nations, creeds, and color are created by God, loved by Him, that Jesus came for all people, and that all are equally influenced and supported their work and the Civil Rights movement in America. The Barnharts' belief in Jesus's teaching on placing God first, serving Him alone, and giving to those in need has led them to distribute millions of dollars and decades of care to the poor, the hungry, and the lost — many of whom they will not meet — all around the world. These are but a few examples. There are countless more. There is still work to be done, no doubt. But let me tell you about the greatest work Jesus did.

This is not a theory to me. It is what I learned that helped me to redefine my life and my leadership and influenced a lot of the principles of this book. Jesus Christ, the man that lived on Earth, who lived the life I could not live: a perfect life. He was completely righteous, he gave himself up and sacrificed himself and died. He gave up his life so that you and I could be reconnected and could be saved. That each of us could be saved from all of our brokenness and the brokenness of this world that we're all so desperately trying to fix. He died so that through His death, and His resurrection, yes, he rose, from the dead. He died so that through His resurrection, He could reestablish that relationship and through Him redefine it all. Our relationship with God, our lives, forever. He knew we could never earn it, so he made a way — The Way — and made it available to all who put their faith in Him.

I told you it was even greater than my leadership transformation. Immeasurably more. It happened that this faith journey paralleled my leadership journey, and was, is, and will forever be even more impactful than my leadership transformation. The old is gone, the new has come — forever to be replaced, and everything in my life has been amplified since I went all in.

If you're interested. If you want to learn more. The Bible is the best place to start, and a good place to start is in the book of Mark. If you have questions. Give me a call. It would be a great joy to speak with you. My phone number is 832-895-1253.

Is faith something that is important to you?

If you have faith that the bright, beautiful future you see possible will benefit your neighbor, your community, or the world when you and others serve the *mission first, people always* with sincerity and Skill. It's time to serve. To act. To lead. Redefine your servant leadership and you may just redefine the world.

And, I hope you do.

But even if you don't redefine *the* world, it will redefine *your* world.

My world was shattered when I left my boss's office. Their feedback about my conflict avoidance and its impact on my integrity was a defining moment. It was the moment I decided to replace the impossible, worn out, and untrue ideas I had about how servant leadership had to be. It was when I began the long, challenging, and fulfilling journey of growing my Character, Relationships, and Skills. It was when I saw that willfully giving up some personal standing, my comfort, if it stood in the way of what I hoped to accomplish, actually gave me what I need to truly serve and lead. When I embraced the tension that is servant leadership, I was strengthened to be able to give my highest-level contribution to the mission — to the people, to my family, and to myself.

My prayer for you is that you will choose — gladly — to grow, and that as you grow you experience transformative results in your work and in the relationships with the people you lead. I have seen others experience this, and I know it can happen. I also pray that you receive the freedom, confidence, and joy that comes through the redefining process.

Be well. Lead on!

In service,
Jon

ACKNOWLEDGMENTS

Mom and Dad, I am forever grateful. The example of a life of service you exemplified guides me to this day. Your unwavering belief, support, and encouragement give me what I need, always, to endure. The only things more valuable than those are the unconditional love I feel from you and your faith in Jesus Christ that you display and instilled in me. I love you.

To my family, (Mom, Dad, Meghan, Anna, William, Benjamin, Jeff, Ashley, Emmy, Kennedy, Olivia) my extended family, (Grandma Bathje, Grandma Kidwell, Aunt Sharon, Uncle Don, Aunt Karen, Uncle John, Aunt Sandy, Uncle Scott, Aunt Jody, Uncle Mark, Aunt Christy plus each and every one of my beloved cousins and cousins-in-law (is that a thing? I count you as first cousins!)) — with a special shoutout to Kenz who was the first person to work for Leadwell — and the family I married into (Mike, Joanna, Kris, Carla, Ty, Cole, Max, Katie, Mark, Brittany, Wyatt, and Grandma Wardin plus all of the extended family Muellers and Wardins). You'd be hard-pressed to find a group of people more loving, dedicated, driven to serve others, and who have a do anything, go anywhere attitude for God and the ones you love. I am grateful for the generations of great examples. You are a blessing I cherish. I love you. Thank you.

Thank you to the countless servant leaders who have influenced and impacted my life. While the names are too many to list, please know that, teachers, coaches, colleagues, leaders, pastors, and friends are who are on my mind and in my heart when I express gratitude. If you're in one of those categories — it's you.

Alan and Katherine Barnhart, thank you for choosing to share your story, especially on a Friday night Zoom years ago, and giving me and my family an example of what a God-driven life of service could look like and how to live it out practically. Thank you for allowing me to share a portion of your story to guide and encourage others.

Preston, my mentor, thank you for opening your home. For loving and caring for me and my family in one of our most challenging times. Thank you for the example you set and the Biblically-based wisdom you use to advise me, often. I/we love and cherish you and Susan.

E.J. Schiro, founder of Schiro Creative, designer of the book cover and graphics for this book, and for the Leadwell brand. Your willingness to iterate, tweak, and change course at the drop of a hat are appreciated. Plus, your thoughtful, modern, and simple designs that help bring words and ideas to life. Thank you.

Carolyn Oakley, Luminous Moon Design, thank you for formatting and laying out this book so it serves the reader. Your guidance through the detail of *all* that needs to happen to actually publish is priceless.

Angela Lassandro, my teammate and friend, and cheerleader! You spur me on and level me up with your energetic collaborative style. What you SEE that others don't, that brings about such generous contributions, especially to the myths, amplified this book beyond what I could've done alone. Thank you.

Michelle Auerbach, my writing guru! And sage. And encourager. And tetherer. You helped me take words, blow them up, rearrange, shrink them down, and rearrange again. You redefined the level of this book, and made sure we kept some back for the next book(s). I am grateful for your help. I am more grateful for you. Thank you.

Carla Wardin, my editor, I am proud to be your brother-in-law. Your writing, enthusiasm, competitiveness (where's my invite to return to the Olympics), and your ability to tell the truth, and daring go-getter attitude inspire me more than you can know. Thank you for making this book better, and leaving plenty of my quirks. Thank you!

Steven Knudsen, my best friend (outside of Meg), you allowed me to run this book by you and work out the ideas, almost always at 5:35 am. ;) You are a great roommate, and even better friend. I respect you, admire you, and look to you as you imitate Christ so I can do the same. Thank you for helping me make this book better. Love you, brother. Thanks.

Matthew Jewell, my operations manager, research and writing assistant, assistant, designer, and... the thorn in my side. Which I absolutely love, because you make me and our work that much better — each and every day with each and every question, idea, and rabbit hole. Because of your Herculean effort the book is significantly better, simpler, and more enjoyable (or at least semi-grammatically correct). My thanks cannot be expressed appropriately with merely a thank you. But, THANK YOU!

Anna, William, and Benjamin, my children, thank you for running to me as soon as I step out of the office and wanting to play... every day. Your joy is contagious. I love you. I will always love you. May God always bless you and keep you.

Meghan, my wife, my love, thank you for going all in on me and with me. I love you. You are my best friend, most trusted advisor, my cheerleader, my partner, magnificent mother to our children, and the love of my life. You are an amazing Godly woman. I am the man I am today, and every day, because of you. All my love, now and forever.

REFERENCES

1. Dweck, C. *Mindset: The New Psychology of Success.* Penguin Random House; 2006.

2. Google Search Dictionary. *Definition of Leader.* The Oxford English Dictionary, part of Oxford Languages.
https://www.google.com/search?q=definition+of+leader

3. Dictionary. *Leadership.* Merriam-Webster Dictionary Online.
https://www.merriam-webster.com/dictionary/leadership

4. *Yes Man.* Warner Bros. 2008

5. Tait B. *Traditional Leadership Vs. Servant Leadership.* Forbes. Published 2020.
https://www.forbes.com/sites/forbescoachescouncil/2020/03/11/traditional-leadership-vs-servant-leadership/?sh=21d0920e451e.

6. White SK. *What Is Servant Leadership? A Philosophy for People-First Leadership.* SHRM. Published February 28, 2022. https://www.shrm.org/executive/resources/articles/pages/servant-leadership-.aspx

   Originally Published by CIO Executive Editorial: https://www.cio.com/article/303848/what-is-servant-leadership-a-philosophy-for-people-first-leadership.html

7. Greenleaf RK. *The Servant as Leader.* The Greenleaf Center for Servant Leadership; 1970.

8. Maxwell JC. *The 21 Irrefutable Laws of Leadership.* Thomas Nelson; London; 2008.

9. Lencioni P. *The Motive: Why So Many Leaders Abdicate Their Most Important Responsibilities.* A Leadership Fable. John Wiley & Sons, Inc; 2020.

10. American Bible Society. *Good News Bible: Today's English Version.* American Bible Society; 2000.

11. The Lockman Foundation. *New American Standard Bible.* Zondervan; 2020. (Romans 12:2)

12. Cloud H. *Integrity: The Courage to Meet the Demands of Reality.* Harper; 2009.

13. McClelland, D. C. (1961). *The Achieving Society.* Princeton, NJ: Van Nostrand.

14. John Sims Townsend. *People Fuel: Fill Your Tank for Life, Love, and Leadership.* Zondervan; 2019.

15. Goleman D. *Emotional Intelligence.* Bantam Books; 2007.

16. Covey SR. *7 Habits of Highly Effective People.* Simon & Schuster Ltd; 2020.

17. Berger W. *A More Beautiful Question: The Power of Inquiry to Spark Breakthrough Ideas.* Bloomsbury; 2016.

18. Attributed to Zig Ziglar. *Original Source Unknown.* Date unknown.

19. Jeroen Kraaijenbrink on LinkedIn. *Humble vs. Vulnerable Leadership.* LinkedIn. Accessed August 20, 2023. https://www.linkedin.com/posts/jeroenkraaijenbrink_ leadershipdevelopment-managementdevelopment-activity-7083099291539369984-1SVt/?

20. *Zoolander.* Paramount. 2001.

21. Howard R, Lash J. *This Was Your Life!* Chosen Books; 1998.

22. Collins J. *Good to Great.* Random House; 2001.

23. History.com Editors. *Montgomery Bus Boycott.* History.com. Published February 3, 2010. https://www.history.com/topics/black-history/montgomery-bus-boycott

24. Clear J. *Atomic Habits.* Penguin Publishing Group; 2018.

25. Barnhart. *Mission.* https://www.barnhartcrane.com/about/mission/

26. LinkedIn Company Insights. *Barnhart Crane and Rigging.* LinkedIn. Accessed on August 30, 2023. https://www.linkedin.com/company/barnhart-crane-&-rigging/ insights/

27. Glassdoor. *Glassdoor Reviews.* Glassdoor. https://www.glassdoor.com/Reviews/Barnhart-Crane-and-Rigging-Reviews-E356008.htm

28. Salary.com. *CEO Salary in the United States.* Salary.com. Accessed on August 30, 2023. https://www.salary.com/research/salary/alternate/ceo-salary

29. Whyte LE. *Giving It All.* Philanthropy Roundtable. https://www. philanthropyroundtable.org/magazine/spring-2014-giving-it-all/

Servant Heart. Business Mind.

Your *Impact* grows when you do.

Leaders need a Coach who helps them grow the Character, Relationships, and Skills needed to Amplify their impact as a leader.

A **Leadwell** *Coach* will help you:

> Assess your strengths and overcome challenges

> Transform your leadership presence and influence

> Increase your ability to adapt and respond

> Grow as a *mission first, people always* leader

> Identify targets and reach goals to amplify your impact

Connect with a Coach now at:

LEADWELL.COM/COACHING

LEAD*Well*

Equipping mission-driven leaders through training and coaching